70 TIMELESS QUOTES AND SAYINGS

70 TIMELESS QUOTES AND SAYINGS

WORDS THAT CAN MAKE YOUR LIFE BETTER, EASIER, AND HAPPIER

Thomas R. Morris

Simple Logic Publications

70 TIMELESS QUOTES AND SAYINGS

Copyright © 2016 and 2023 Thomas R. Morris All rights reserved. No part of this book may be reproduced or transmitted by any means or in any form without prior written consent of the author. This includes photocopying, scanning, storing in or transmitting by any computer-based device or system.

The author and publisher of this book make no claim of copyright in any of the quotes in this book. However, the author's comments or interpretation of the quotes is copyright protected.

Disclaimer: This book has been created for general reference and is intended merely to provide thoughts and motivation regarding the subject matter covered. This book is sold with the full understanding that the author and publisher are not engaged in rendering psychological advice of any kind. The author and the publisher disclaim any and all liability and shall not be liable for any loss personal or otherwise, or any consequences or damages whatsoever, direct or indirect, as a result of the use of any of the quotes or comments that are provided in this book. The author and publisher of this book assume no responsibility for any inaccuracies, inconsistencies, errors or omissions that may appear. The contents of this book are the sole expression and opinion of its author and not necessarily that of the publisher. No guarantees or warranties are expressed or implied by the author or the publisher.

For more information, please contact the publisher at:
information@simplelogicpublications.com
Please note that we do not accept unsolicited manuscripts.

Illustrations under license from shutterstock.com,
istockphoto.com, and adobe.com

ISBN 978-0-9954007-8-8 (Trade Paperback)
(Original work published 2016 as *Life's Secrets* ISBN 978-0-9872677-5-7)
Printed in Australia, the United Kingdom, and
the United States of America

Table of Contents

Introduction..1
PART 1　　　　　　KNOWLEDGE　　　　　　3
  1 Benjamin Franklin..5
  2 Socrates..7
  3 Marcus Aurelius..9
  4 Epictetus...11
  5 Ralph Waldo Emerson..13
  6 Francis Bacon...15
  7 Ralph Waldo Emerson..17
  8 Aesop..19
  9 Plutarch..21
PART 2　　　　　　LIFE　　　　　　23
  10 Johann Wolfgang von Goethe..25
  11 Euripides..27
  12 Confucius...29
  13 Henry David Thoreau..31
  14 Michelangelo...33
  15 Abraham Lincoln..35
  16 Lucius Annaeus Seneca..37
  17 Epictetus...39
  18 Ralph Waldo Emerson...41
  19 Victor Hugo...43
  20 Horace...45
  21 Mark Twain...47
  22 Epictetus...49
  23 Lao Tzu..51
  24 Henry David Thoreau..53
PART 3　　　　　　SELF　　　　　　55
  25 Ralph Waldo Emerson...57
  26 François de La Rochefoucauld..59
  27 Buddha...61
  28 Epictetus...63
  29 Socrates..65
  30 Rudolf Steiner...67

31	Johann Wolfgang von Goethe	69
32	Soren Kierkegaard	71
PART 4	HAPPINESS	73
33	Aristotle	75
34	François de La Rochefoucauld	77
35	Marcus Aurelius	79
36	Johann Wolfgang von Goethe	81
37	Democritus	83
38	Buddha	85
39	Lucius Annaeus Seneca	87
40	Confucius	89
PART 5	MAKING THINGS HAPPEN	91
41	William Shakespeare	93
42	Mark Twain	95
43	Confucius	97
44	Lao Tzu	99
45	Epictetus	101
46	Victor Hugo	103
47	Virgil	105
48	Lao Tzu	107
49	Vincent Van Gogh	109
50	Marcus Aurelius	111
51	Johann Wolfgang von Goethe	113
52	Ralph Waldo Emerson	115
53	William Henley	117
54	Confucius	119
55	Francis Bacon	121
56	Demosthenes	123
57	Alexander Graham Bell	125
58	John Pym Abraham Lincoln	127
59	Miyamoto Musashi	129
60	Alexander the Great	131
61	Benjamin Franklin	133
PART 6	OLD SAYINGS	135
BIOGRAPHIES		155

Introduction

Things in life might not be the way we want them to be. It may be that our relationships or finances are a mess. Maybe we feel that we don't fit in with those we want to fit in with or we have problems with those we are with. Or it might be that we aren't making enough money to live how we really want to live our life. It could be that we never seem to be able to accomplish anything. Maybe we feel that we never get the break we need that would enable us to get ahead in life. It could be that we are always stressed out. Or it might be that we aren't happy with who we have become and our life isn't how we had hoped it would be.

There are many reasons why life can be tough, and the why varies from person to person. Maybe it's because we have the wrong attitude (the wrong way of looking at things) or that we made a few too many bad choices or decisions in our life. It might be because of things we did or said that weren't the right things to do or say. It could be because of things we didn't do or say that we should have done or said. It may be because we hate our job or lack the skills that would enable us to get a better job. It might be because we hang out with the wrong people or chose the wrong person (husband or wife) to spend our life with. Whatever the reasons may be, things just aren't the way we would like them to be.

Why things are the way they are is often because we didn't know what we needed to know when we needed to know it – life's secrets, shortcuts, skills, techniques and knowledge that can help us to make our life better, easier, and happier.

Hundreds, even thousands, of years ago, some really smart people spoke of or wrote down many of these secrets, shortcuts, skills, techniques, and knowledge. All of these things can help us today to make our life easier, better, and happier. They can help us to get to where we want to be in life – faster and with fewer setbacks.

This book sets out 70 quotes or sayings by people who have all done extraordinary things in and with their lives. Each is followed by a short commentary to help get the reader started – to think about each quote or saying and decide for themselves how it could help them to get what they truly want in their life.

Over one hundred years ago, Mark Twain wrote:

The secret of getting ahead is getting started.

Taking just a few minutes each day starting today to read and think about one quote or saying and the short commentary in this book could make your life easier, better and happier. No better time to start than now.

All quotes in this book have been widely attributed to the names that appear under each quote. Both the author and publisher take no responsibility for inaccuracies.

PART 1
Knowledge

Learning is a treasure that will follow its owner everywhere.

(Chinese proverb)

1

An investment in knowledge always pays the best interest.

(Benjamin Franklin 1706 – 1790)

Knowledge plays a role in pretty much everything we do in life. It can help us to make better choices and decisions. It can help us to set better goals and to create effective plans and strategies that will enable us to achieve those goals. It can help us to deal with the things life throws at us, and to fix things that aren't working in our life. The more we know, the more we can be rewarded (the *more interest* we are paid) for what we know.

Knowledge can enable us to improve our self-esteem and self-confidence. It helps us to take better care of our health. It can enable us to create or find an income source (job) that's *perfect* for us. This includes being able to earn as much money as we desire. Knowledge also helps us to make friends with those who are right for us, find the right partner, and to be a better friend and partner.

Knowledge gives us the power to take control of our life, as it provides us with what we need to know in order to become who we we truly wish to be and to create and live a healthy, happy, and satisfying life. What better reward (*interest*) is there than that?

The best way to invest in knowledge is through self-education. Self-education means – we choose what we study. To choose what we study, we need to determine who we wish to become and what we wish to do in and with our life. Once we have done that, we can determine what we need to know to make it happen. Then it's up to us to gain that knowledge and put that knowledge into action. Walt Disney and Al Pacino *didn't* finish high school. Bill Gates and Lady Gaga *didn't* finish college. (To name only a few) They're all self-educated – learned what they needed to know to get what they wanted.

2

To know is to know that you know nothing. That is the meaning of true knowledge.

(Socrates 469 BC – 399 BC)

To know is to know that you know nothing could mean that in order to acquire true knowledge, we must first know (acknowledge) that what we may think or believe we know may in fact not be what or how things really are.

Dictionaries define *knowledge* as information or skills known that have been acquired through experience or education by perceiving, discovering or learning. The problem with such a definition is – this experience and education is influenced and shaped by our *perception*. In other words, the knowledge we acquire is influenced and shaped by what we think and believe and how we feel about people and things. This could mean that the knowledge we gain through experience and education is subjective and thus is merely our opinion. Opinion is not necessarily knowing nor is it true knowledge.

Socrates may be telling us that rather than go through life thinking that what we think or believe is the truth, we need to admit to ourselves that what we think or believe we know may in fact not be true. It could be that he is telling us that we need to be willing to let go of our perceptions and to be on a continual search for the real truth, the irrefutable truths and facts about life and the universe. In other words, we need to be open minded to discover what and how things *really are*.

It's not what we may think or believe something is that gets us what we want in life, but rather it's what things actually are. True knowledge is likely to give us a much better chance of becoming who we truly wish to be, living our life the way we truly wish to live it.

3

Everything we hear is an opinion, not a fact. Everything we see is a perspective, not the truth.

(Marcus Aurelius 121 – 180)

Although there are inherent facts and truths about life and the universe, so much of what we hear and see is merely opinion or perception. Opinion and perception are not necessarily fact or the truth. Rather they are interpretations of something someone sees, hears, smells, touches or tastes. It's what's real to them, what something seems to be, but not necessarily what it really is.

An opinion is a belief, view or judgment about or appraisal of something, not necessarily based on fact or true knowledge. It is a subjective conclusion that one has made about something they saw, heard, smelled, touched or tasted. There is personal, group, public, expert and even scientific opinion (some of which may be supported by facts and principles) but all continue to be an opinion until proven to be fact or the truth.

Perception is the result of the mental process of interpreting sensory stimuli (sight, sound, smell, touch and taste) in order to explain and better understand things. It's a mental image of a sensory experience. Perception is influenced or shaped by things like thoughts, beliefs, feelings, attitudes, expectations and past experiences of the person who has perceived. In other words, perception is subjective and, like opinion, isn't necessarily how or what things really are.

Every day we are bombarded by opinion, perception, hype, exaggeration, falsehoods, conspiracy theories and senseless information. To become who we truly want to be and to get and live the life we really want, we need to hear and see beyond all of it and find the facts and the truth, and use that to get what we want.

4

It is impossible to begin to learn that which one thinks one already knows.

(Epictetus 55 – 135)

Thinking that we already know something can stop us from learning. Thinking that we already know can stop us from looking at things from a different perspective, opening our mind to new ideas, and experiencing new things. Thinking that we already know can prevent us from adjusting, improving and even correcting what we might think we know. When we think we already know, we can stop ourselves from learning more about what and how things really are; discovering the truth.

Thinking that we already know something can stop us from knowing that we don't know. It can stop us from thinking about what we think we know, thus stop us from determining if there is room for improvement in what we know, which very likely there always will be.

Thinking that we already know something can lead to making excuses or blaming others for our problems. This can mean that we deny the need to fix or change things or what we need to fix or change. It can stop us from listening to people, people who may have something valuable to offer us. It can stop us learning about other cultures and from overcoming our prejudices and biases. Thinking that we already know something can stop us from learning what we need to know – things that could enable us to become who we truly wish to be living the life we really want.

Know that you don't know it all. Know that you don't have all the answers. Know that to learn we must not think that we already know. Know that the more we learn, the happier we will be and the more rewarding and satisfying our life can be.

5

Unless you try to do something beyond what you have already mastered, you will never grow.

(Ralph Waldo Emerson 1803 – 1882)

To be alive means to grow. To get the most out of life, we need to grow. This means that we need to stretch ourselves; try new things, take (calculated) risks, take on challenges and find, create and act on opportunities. These are things that can help us to make changes in ourselves and in our life, to grow. These are things that can enable us to become who we really wish to be and to get us what we truly desire in life – to truly be alive.

Trying new things, taking risks, taking on challenges and acting on opportunities brings excitement into our life. Excitement encourages us to jump out of our box, to step out of our comfort zone to discover what's out there. Discovery often means new places. New places often means seeing and experiencing new things. New things can enable us to learn more, to continue to grow. New places can often mean meeting new people. New people can mean new ideas and new ideas help us to grow.

Don't settle for who you are now. Do more to become more. Don't settle for where you are in life today. Do more so that you can get where you really want to be. To get the most out of life, we need to continue to grow throughout our life. This means that we need to do and master new things, things beyond those that we have already done and mastered.

Goals can enable us to do so. Setting and achieving short, medium and long term goals throughout our life enables us to do more in our life. It's positive results and outcomes from these goals that will enable us to get the most out of our life and to truly be alive.

6

Knowledge is power.

(Francis Bacon 1561 – 1626)

Today this should read *The right knowledge is power*. With the arrival of the Internet, we now have quick and easy access to massive amounts of information about everything. A lot of that information is subjective and speculative, and some is inaccurate, even simply incorrect. Such information can distort what one knows, one's knowledge. Such knowledge can lead to power but not true long lasting power – positive energy having a positive impact on our mental, physical and social health.

The *right* knowledge enables us to make better choices and decisions. It enables us to create better and more effective plans and strategies that enable us to achieve our goals. The right knowledge enables us to increase our abilities, skills, and potential. It can also enable us to create or improve our reputation and influence, and even gain the respect and admiration of others. When we possess the right knowledge, our chances of succeeding in whatever we do is certain to increase. All of this can enable us (give us the power) to get what we need and desire in life.

We gain power from knowledge when the knowledge we possess enables us to do what we wish to do in and with our life. We gain power when the knowledge we possess enables us to do what other people are unable to do or to do it a little better than others. This enables us to charge more for our time (work) thereby giving us power over time and money – the power to work less and earn more. More time and money can enable us to do more of the things we want to do in our life, and to protect our future and well-being.

7

Before we acquire great power we must acquire wisdom to use it well.

(Ralph Waldo Emerson 1803 – 1882)

Power means different things to different people. For Lao Tzu, *Mastering others is strength. Mastering yourself is true power.* For Seneca, *Most powerful is he who has himself in his own power.* Emerson wrote about self-reliance, the power (ability) to determine who we become and what we do and get in our life – *self-determination*. The greater the power, the more control we have of the direction we take in our life – more freedom.

Self-determination is a mindset and desire to *master ourselves*, not others. It inspires us to identify the things we need to fix, improve or change in ourselves. When we have done so, we will want to do whatever we need to do to fix, improve or change those things. Self-determination *empowers us* to protect ourselves from adverse pressure or influence by others and society, as we will wish to maintain maximum control of our life. When we do maintain control, we think for ourselves, live our life based on our own set of beliefs, values and standards, make our own choices and decisions and set and achieve our own goals. All of this enables us to create and live the life we desire.

Wisdom means having the ability to apply good judgment and insight. It's knowing how to take control of our life; how to make the right decisions, set the right goals and know the best action to take that will lead to optimal results and outcomes. It's optimal results and outcomes that enable us to create and live the life of our dreams – to become who we really wish to be and do what we truly wish to do in and with our life. When we can do that, we have acquired great power.

8

Better be wise by the misfortunes of others than by your own.

(Aesop 621 BC – 564 BC)

We can save ourselves a lot of time, energy, money, heartache, stress and even our life simply by observing the mistakes and misfortunes of others. The things we observe can greatly reduce *life's learning curve*. In other words, we don't have to experience it ourselves or put in time and effort trying to figure it out for ourselves.

Observing the mistakes or misfortunes of others could help us to avoid potential risks, challenges, obstacles, mistakes or setbacks. It could enable us to avoid pain or suffering. It may enable us to recognize something we may have otherwise missed or had not known existed. It could demonstrate how or how not to do something in order to get the best results and outcomes. It could provide us with the knowledge of a better way to do things or an easier or quicker way to do them.

We can learn from what others have said or didn't say, did or didn't do, or something that happened or didn't happen. All it takes is to listen, watch and observe, and have an open mind; to be objective and recognize what led to the mistake or misfortune.

When we are faced with a difficult task or challenge, wish to take on a new challenge or opportunity, or are dealing with something life has thrown at us, we can learn from the experiences of others. Those we know or don't know who have made mistakes or experienced misfortune in their attempt to do or get the same or similar things we need or want, may have the answers or solutions we need in order to do or get what we truly desire. Our parents, partner and close friends can be a great place to start, to learn from their experiences.

9

Know how to listen, and you will profit even from those who talk badly.

(Plutarch 46 – 120)

We can learn something from pretty much anyone. It might be our parents or friends, or it may be someone who disagrees with us or criticizes us for what we think, believe, feel or do. It could be someone from a different culture or subculture or maybe a politician we disagree with. It could even be the guy down the street who we think is an imbecile. The key is to *know how to listen* (and in some cases when to stop listening and walk away).

To hear what others are saying, we need to concentrate on the words and message, not the person. We need to take the time to listen and to be patient to hear what they are really saying. We need to stay objective, that is, not allow our emotions to influence what we hear or to distort what is really being said. To help us to do so, we need to keep in mind that what others say is often simply their thoughts or opinion. And although what they say may not be what we think, believe or feel, it *may* offer information that we could learn/profit from.

We need to let the conversation flow, that is, to resist interrupting or firing back with counter arguments. We should ask questions if we feel that it will provide us with information that will enable us to better understand the message that person is trying to convey. We need to hear the real message so that we can consider and possibly learn from what has been said.

Knowing how to listen, to listen *effectively*, is a skill we all need to learn. Effective listening is a powerful tool useful in everything we experience and do in our life. To hear what has actually been said can help us to get what we really want in life; at work, home and play.

PART 2
Life

Life is short, and it gets shorter each day.

(Anonymous)

10

Nothing is worth more than this day.

(Johann Wolfgang von Goethe 1749 – 1832)

Yesterday is gone forever and tomorrow might never come. Today is the day to live life. Today is the day to be happy and to do the things we enjoy doing. Today is the day to smile, laugh, love, take care of our health and to help others to do the same.

Today is the day to appreciate the people in our life and to tell and show those we love how we feel. Today is the day to hug our partner, a friend, our dog or cat or just hug ourselves. Rain or shine, today is a beautiful day to be lived to the fullest.

Today is also the day that will shape our tomorrow, so today is the day to improve ourselves. Today is the day to learn something new and to try something we have not done before. Today is the day to be a good person and do something good for someone we know, or may not know, which might just make their day.

Today is the day to discover who we really want to be and what we really want in and from our life. Today is the day to start or continue to take positive action that will enable us to get what we really want in life.

Don't waste today fretting about yesterday. Live your life today and use today to benefit from the things you learned yesterday. Don't waste your today worrying about tomorrow. Do something positive today. Doing so is caring for your tomorrow.

Don't forget to live. Have and maintain a *live life in the present* mindset. Doing so is certain to ensure that we truly experience life, that we are living the journey not simply waiting to arrive at the destination.

11

There is just one life for each of us; our own.

(Euripides 480 BC – 406 BC)

To be truly happy and satisfied in life, we need to be: healthy, who we truly wish to be, and doing what we truly enjoy and want to do in and with our life. Trying to live our life like others will stop us from being and doing exactly that.

We all think, believe and feel differently. We have all seen and experienced different things in our life. Our brain has interpreted those things differently, based on what we think, believe and feel. Choices, decisions, and goals that are right for us are those based on who we are, who we wish to become and what we desire in life.

We are all different. Some things just feel right for us and other things don't. What makes others happy and satisfied might not do the same for us. The goals and aspirations of others are likely to be different, at least they are unlikely to be exactly the same as ours.

Don't waste your life trying to be someone you aren't. Don't waste your life trying to live your life the way your friends or neighbors are living theirs. Don't waste your life trying to meet the benchmarks or criteria set by others, society, the media, marketing or advertising.

Life offers us all a fantastic opportunity to *custom build* our life. We can imagine and create a life that will make us truly happy and satisfied with our life, during and at the end of our life.

Take the time and make the effort today to discover who *you really want* to become and what *you really want* in life. Then start today doing whatever you need to do to make it happen, to live a life that's perfect *for you*.

12

Life is actually really simple, but we insist on making it complicated.

(Confucius 551 BC – 479 BC)

Not knowing the difference between need and desire may be the main reason many people's lives aren't so simple. To desire is to be preoccupied with the future and thus reducing one's ability to live in the present. For some of us, this could mean we spend our life desiring more or something better in life rather than spend that time doing what needs to be done today to have it.

Desire can complicate the heart, mind and soul. Desire for something could mean that we need to work more to earn more to buy whatever it may be. It may mean going into debt. Either way, this makes life *less simple*. The desire for someone or to please someone can lead us to be someone we aren't or doing things we would not otherwise do. This is certain to *complicate our life*.

Not being in control of one's life may be the next major reason many people's lives aren't so simple. Not being in control can mean we fail to make our own decisions or take positive action on the decisions we do make. This can mean that we don't get the things we need in life. Lack of money or even too much money can also make our life complicated. So too can having too many "friends" on social media sites, or living with someone who carries with them excess baggage from their past.

An uncomplicated life is a happier and healthier life. We need to know what we are going to do before we do it so that what we do doesn't complicate our life. Take marriage, for instance. Before marrying someone, we need to know who that person *really* is. We also need to know about the sacrifices that come with being married and any excess baggage they will bring with them.

13

The price of anything is the amount of life you exchange for it.

(Henry David Thoreau 1817 – 1862)

Our time is our life. When we work, we exchange our time (*part of our life*) for money. When we do something, we exchange time and energy to do it. The more time we need in order to have (pay for) or do something, the more life we need to exchange in order to have or do it.

When we buy something, the price we pay is the time it took us to earn the money (after income tax) to buy it. When we do something, the price we pay is not only time and energy spent doing it, it's also the cost of the opportunity lost; exchanging that time and energy for something rather than exchanging it for something else.

Life is the most valuable commodity. Without people willing to exchange their life for the things they want to have or do, there would likely be no trade of goods or services, no jobs and even a lack of activity in life. We can't buy more *life time*. The older we get, the less time we have. The less time we have, the less life we have to exchange. The less life we have to exchange, the more valuable our time (life) is (should be) to us.

To live the life we truly desire, we must value our time and know *how best to exchange our life time.* This means that we need to know what we truly need to be happy and satisfied in life. It means that we need to use our time to increase our knowledge and skills so that we can earn more and use less of our time to do so. It also means that we need to be aware of the methods people use to persuade us to buy things and pressure us into doing things so that we don't waste our life time buying things we don't really need or doing things we don't want to do.

14

The greater danger for most of us lies not in setting our aim too high and falling short; but in setting our aim too low, and achieving our mark.

(Michelangelo 1475 – 1564)

If we expect less, chances are we will get less. When we expect more, we usually get more. To become who we dream of being living the life we dream of living, we need to expect a lot from ourselves and our life. Then we need to achieve what we expect.

Achieving high expectations encourages us to achieve even more. When we achieve what we aimed for, we are likely to feel that it was well worth the time and energy we put in to achieving it. This is likely to lead us to aim for even more with even higher expectations.

To achieve high aims and goals, we need to:

- Believe that we deserve to get and have what we are aiming for.
- Aim for that which is just a little higher than what we might think or believe we are able to achieve, rather than beneath it.
- Ensure that our aims and goals are realistic. This means we need to currently have or can acquire the knowledge, skills or time needed to do whatever is required to achieve those aims and goals.
- Create and carry out effective plans and strategies that will enable us to achieve those aims and goals.
- Not let anyone (*including ourselves*) to convince us that we can't or won't achieve what we are aiming to achieve.

The only one who stops us from achieving great things in ourselves and in our life – is ourselves. Aim high and do whatever it takes to achieve what you aim for.

15

**In the end, it's not the years
in your life that count.
It's the life in your years.**

(Abraham Lincoln 1809 – 1865)

Some people do and achieve so much in life. Perhaps they have a loving family and spend a lot of time with their family. Maybe they reach the top of their profession or create a very successful business. It may be that they mentor others and help those in need. It could be that they travel the world, meet new people, experience new cultures, and maybe learn to speak a new language or two. They are healthy, honest, financially secure, and truly enjoy doing what they do at home, work and play.

When we reach the end of our *life journey*, chances are we will regret not doing the things we wished we had done more than we will regret the things we did do that we wished we hadn't done. Don't wait for "someday" or wait until you have "more time", and definitely don't wait until you retire to do the things you want to do in your life. Find or create a way to *do it as soon as you can*. The sooner you do the things you want to do, the more time you will have to do even more. Putting off doing something for some day in the future *could mean* that you never get to do it.

Life may be short for some and longer for others, but what one has done in their life does determine if they have really lived life. Setting goals, creating plans and strategies that will enable us to achieve those goals, and doing whatever it takes to carry out those plans and strategies enables us to do and achieve so much in our life. Today is the day to start living your life to the fullest – each and every day. Today is the day to set and to achieve goals, to fill your years with the things you really wish to do in your life.

16

It is quality rather than quantity that matters.

(Lucius Annaeus Seneca 4 BC – 65 AD)

Quality is how someone or something is; a personal trait, characteristic, property, attribute, grade, standard, or degree of excellence. *Quantity* is the amount or number of something, how much – its size, weight or volume.

It's quality, not quantity, that determines whether we are *truly happy* in life.

- A circle of a few good friends, those of good character, is more important than the number of friends. (Quality friends leads to more meaningful and satisfying relationships.)

- An hour of time when we are focused on and dedicated to what we are doing is more valuable than hours of idle or wasted time. (Quality time enables us to give full attention to what we are doing, which often leads to better, quicker, and more satisfying results.)

- A smaller amount of healthy food and exercise is better than a larger amount of junk food and inactivity. (Quality food and exercise keeps us healthy.)

- Occasional *passionate fun* sex (quality) is more gratifying than daily/nightly mediocre or lousy sex.

- A shorter life of health and true happiness is surely better than a longer life of poor health and misery.

Labels, titles, size, even price doesn't necessarily mean quality. More is not always better. Too many friends, too many material things, too much wasted or idle time, too much food, even too much money, exercise or sex can take us down, as too many or too much can consume us, harm our body and complicate our life.

17

In order to please others, we loose our hold on our life's purpose.

(Epictetus 55 – 135)

Our main purpose in life, next to staying alive, is to be truly happy. True happiness is found when we are who we wish to be living a life that enables us to fulfill our dreams and desires. This requires that we are in control of our life.

Some people are so preoccupied with pleasing others that they lose control. To please others, they may allow others to influence, even determine, what they think and believe and how they feel. They may allow others to make their choices and decisions for them. They may also allow other people to set the direction they end up going in life – maybe doing things that aren't right for them.

Peer pressure can influence what we do in life. It can get us to say *Yes* when we really want to say *No*. It can get us to do things we don't want to do. It can put us in places where we don't want to be. Peer pressure can stop us from pursuing what we really wish to do in and with our life. It can change the course of our life simply because we wish to please others rather than stand up for what we believe is right and best for us. We might not even know what is right or best for us.

Social pressure can influence what we do with our life. It can keep us from recognizing who we are becoming or have become and what we are doing with our life. This can prevent us from fixing or changing things in ourselves and in our life that stop us from fulfilling our life purpose. Being how we are *supposed* to be – to please others (society), can easily take us in a direction we really don't wish to go in life.

18

Do not go where the path may lead, go instead where there is no path and leave a trail.

(Ralph Waldo Emerson 1803 – 1882)

It's easy to simply live life, to go where the path may lead. It doesn't take much to want what others want, to be just like everyone else. But life provides us all with an opportunity to create a unique life, a life of our own. Creating our own life enables us to determine who we become and what we do in our life. It can enable us to do truly amazing things in and with our life. Life is an opportunity to do something that has never been done before or create something that never existed before.

Doing as others do, following the path that others are on or have traveled, may get us what others will get or have gotten in life. But doing so could mean that we fail to recognize, develop and utilize any special talents, skills, abilities or strengths we may have. These special talents, skills, abilities or strengths, our uniqueness, *may* enable us to do something really special in our life.

Taking control of our life gives us the power to think, believe, feel and do things the way *we determine* is best for us. It enables us to choose and decide for ourselves and to set goals that will get us what we really want in life. It enables us to make things happen the way we want things to happen in our life.

When we take control of our life, we will trust and rely on ourselves to think for ourselves. We will discover who we truly wish to be and what we truly wish to do in and with our life. We will discover, develop and take advantage of our uniqueness; use any special talents, skills, abilities and strengths that we do find. We will want to utilize our uniqueness to create our own path, to be an innovator rather than a follower.

19

There is nothing like a dream to create the future.

(Victor Hugo 1802 – 1885)

A dream is an idea or vision voluntarily created in our imagination of something of beauty or excellence. Or it may be of a desired purpose, goal or thing that we wish to achieve or acquire, something that when achieved or acquired completely satisfies a wish or desire.

Not to be mistaken for dreams we experience when we are sleeping (involuntarily activity in our mind), our imagination gives us the power to; live outside the box, forget about reality, let go of the norms, expectations and criteria set by others. When we *voluntarily* dream, we can let our imagination go wild, escape into our mind to *discover* things we never thought about before and to *see* things that never existed before.

Dreaming is a personal time when we can brainstorm with ourselves. It's a time to think about and visualize the impossible and to discover how we can make the impossible possible. It's dreams that put the first man on the moon. Walt Disney's Disneyland is proof of the power of dreaming.

Our dreams can be our eyes into our future, the future we could have if we create goals that would bring about our dreams. If we then do what we need to do to achieve those goals, we could live our dreams.

Take time to dream. Sit down and let your imagination go wild. Don't allow others to stop you from dreaming. *Without dreams, dreams can't come true*. If we don't have dreams to come true, we are missing an exciting and amazing future we could have created for ourselves. Dream big and continue to dream. Create a future filled with the things from your wildest imagination.

20

Remember when life's path is steep, keep your mind even.

(Horace 65 BC – 8 BC)

When life is tough or isn't the way we want it to be, (when life's path is steep) we can *lose control* of our emotions. Losing control of our emotions has a negative effect on our judgment. This can often lead us to react rather than to act.

To *react* is to respond to something that has happened or hasn't happened. A response often takes place without the issue or problem being given much thought. Reacting often *doesn't* resolve the issue or problem. In fact, it can often make things tougher or worse. To *act*, on the other hand, is to take control (keep our mind even) – so that we can think about an issue or problem with the aim of finding a solution. This solution may enable us to fix, overcome or get what we want.

Whether we react or act can have a decisive effect on the choices and decisions we make. These choices and decisions will in turn determine the actions we take. The *right* actions can enable us to prevent, control or correct things that would otherwise make our life's path steep.

To keep our mind even, we need to recognize, understand and remain in control of our emotions. To do so, we need to know what triggers our emotions. Once we do, we need to believe in ourselves that we can survive, overcome, fix or change the things that aren't the way we would like them to be. When we can do this, we can choose to avoid people, places, activities or situations that could set off our triggers. It also enables us to be better prepared to handle and deal with those people, places, activities or situations that we can't avoid so that we can remain in control when our life's path is steep.

21

The lack of money is the root of all evil.

(Mark Twain 1835 – 1910)

Many have claimed that money is the root of all evil. On the contrary, the *lack of money* (or lust for it) is the root of all evil. Not having enough money (or lusting for more) can lead to lying, cheating, deceiving, stealing or doing things one would probably rather not do, in order to have money to get the things one needs or desires.

A good person might lie on tax day so to keep a few extra dollars from their pay. An honest man may steal a loaf of bread to feed his family because he didn't have the money to pay. A person may sell drugs, enter into an undesirable profession or even kill people in order to have the money they need to survive.

A lack of money can can prevent us from learning the skills we need to earn a good income. It can exclude us from getting the education we need or desire and thus reduce our chances of earning enough money to have what we need and desire. It can steal time from us; the time we need to spend doing things that money would have enabled us to do easier or quicker. It can also have a negative effect on how we feel about ourselves.

A lack of money is often the consequence of not knowing what one needs to know that would have enabled them to have enough money. To really live life, we need to gain the knowledge and the skills we need that will enable us to earn enough money so that we can have and do the things we need and want in our life. We also need to gain the knowledge and the skills that will enable us to earn an income doing something that makes us feel good about ourselves. This is likely to contribute to living a good, honest, happy and satisfying life.

22

It's not what happens to you, but how you react to it that matters.

(Epictetus 55 – 135)

When something happens to us, our brain triggers a *response* in our body to what we have just encountered or experienced. This response will lead to an associated emotion. For instance, when we experience something we like or enjoy, our brain triggers a smile (*response*) and that smile makes us feel happy (*associated emotion*).

Our emotions will stimulate us to act or react. When we experience an emotion, that emotion will influence and can have an effect on what and how we feel. What and how we feel often leads to an emotional response from us, an action or reaction, such as hugging someone (action) or lashing out at someone (reaction).

When we act, changes are that we are more likely to think about what has happened or hasn't happened *before* we act. Doing so is likely to enable us to handle or deal with an emotion in a way that will get us a better result. But if we react, we are more likely not to think about it, and thus may fail to effectively deal with or overcome the things that triggered the emotion.

To create and live the life we truly desire, we need to act and avoid reacting to the things that happen to us. This means that we need to understand our emotions and to be in control of our emotions so that we don't respond emotionally to those things. This enables us to control if or how the things people say or do or what we see, experience or what happens to and around us does or doesn't influence or have a negative effect on us or our life. This enables us to do what we need to do (*to take action*) to ignore, deal with, overcome, fix or change whatever it may be that could otherwise do so.

23

If you do not change direction, you may end up where you are heading.

(Lao Tzu 604 BC – 531 BC)

Some people become complacent with their life. They stay in their comfort zone, aren't interested in change. They stop challenging themselves, and may stop taking care of their health, relationships, career and education. They simply accept things the way they have become. Their dreams just fizzle out. They stop making things happen in their life and merely watch life happen to them. They simply go where life takes them.

Some people have taken the wrong direction. Maybe the environment or people they hung out with wasn't right for them. It might be that they were trying to be someone they weren't so to please others. It could be they allowed others to make their decisions for them. Or maybe it's because they failed to listen to their inner voice or simply failed to think before they acted.

Living the life we want – being who we truly wish to be doing the things we really want to do in our life, requires that we change things in ourselves and in our life *when* changes are needed. If we don't change things, things are likely to remain the same. Things could even get worse. Take for instance, if we eat unhealthy food and fail to exercise – failing to change (to eat better and exercise) is likely to result in poor health, even an early death.

Change will enable you to determine and control the direction of your life. If you are currently living the life you *don't* want, now is the time to change direction – to stop, fix, improve or change the things that aren't the way you want them to be. To live the life you *do want*, you need to identify what you need and want to change and then find a way to change it – before it's too late.

24

Go confidently in the direction of your dreams. Live the life you have imagined.

(Henry David Thoreau 1817 – 1862)

Our dreams are our thoughts and visions of who and what we wish to become and what we wish to do and get in our life. These dreams can motivate us and lead us to set into motion the actions we need to take so that we can become, do and get what we desire in life. Our dreams can inspire us to set and achieve goals and to accomplish a purpose in life – to live the life we have imagined for ourselves.

Without action, our dreams simply remain dreams. To make our dreams come true, we must have confidence in ourselves that we can make those dreams come true. Confidence is believing in ourselves. It's believing that we are capable of achieving what we set out to do. It's also believing that *we deserve* to become who and what we want to be and to do and have what we want in life.

Those who fail to realize their dreams are often those who lack confidence in themselves. They may fear that they might not realize their dreams and thus give up or don't even try to make their dreams come true. It may also be that they have allowed others to persuade them to give up on their dreams, being convinced that their dreams are no more than a dream.

Confidence with the right attitude, a positive attitude, enables us to overcome challenges or obstacles that may otherwise stop us from creating and living the life we have imagined for ourselves. Confidence and the right attitude increases our *determination*. Determination provides us with the power we need to prevent others from quashing our dreams. Confidence, the right attitude and action enables us to live the life we dream of living.

PART 3
Self

The snow goose need not bathe to make itself white. Neither need you do anything but be yourself.

(Lao Tzu 604 BC – 531 BC)

25

To be yourself in a world that is constantly trying to make you something else is the greatest accomplishment.

(Ralph Waldo Emerson 1803 – 1882)

Peer pressure can influence who we are and can have an effect on who we become. It can turn us into someone we aren't doing things that aren't who we really are or want to be. Peer pressure can lead us to change our own beliefs and values, and even change what we think and how we feel. It can stop us from recognizing our uniqueness, which can stop us from being who we really are. It can keep us from developing any special talents, skills or attributes that we may have that could enable us to be or to become who we really wish to be.

The media can influence *even determine* the definitions, standards and rules we use to make sense of the world around us. It can influence *even change* our beliefs about people and how the world works. It can thrust upon us values and criteria that we may use to become who we become and determine how we live our life. The media can (if we allow it) convince us what we are *supposed* to think and believe and what we are *supposed* to do in life.

Marketing and advertising people aim to convince us to believe what they want us to believe. They aim to get us to believe who we are *supposed* to be, how we are *supposed* to feel, how we are *supposed* to live our life, and what we are *supposed* to have in life – to fit in, to be like others or better than others. (*Conveniently*, they offer us things they aim to convince us to believe enables us to be who and do as we are *supposed* to be and do.)

To be yourself, you *must* take full responsibility for and maximum control of your life. This means that you need to determine for yourself who you are and *who you wish to become*, and what you need and truly want in life.

26

We are so accustomed to disguise ourselves to others that in the end we become disguised to ourselves.

(François de La Rochefoucauld 1613 – 1680)

People often judge us based on our outer appearance. *Masks* can enable us to appear to be someone who we feel is better than who we believe we are. Masks enable us to make the desired impression; to look important, successful, sexy or that we fit in.

Masks can be almost anything. It might be the clothes, accessories, even the perfume or cologne we wear. It can be the job we have, titles we hold or the car we drive. All of this may be fine, but these masks can hide our true self *from ourselves*. Over time, by trying to be (fulfill the role of) the person we wish to appear to be, we might convince ourselves that we are someone we aren't.

Lies, even little white lies, may over time become what *we think and believe* is true about ourselves. Those who lie to others about who they are can end up having to continue to live that lie so that they don't have to admit that they lied. It might be a lie about one's academic or professional qualifications. Or it might be a lie of one's past or experiences. Much of *who we think we are* is determined by what our subconscious believes. Messages (*lies about ourselves*) that are repeatedly sent to our subconscious may convince our subconscious are true.

Masks and lies can be an ego-defense or self-protection mechanism to protect ourselves from disappointment in who we have become – to protect our self-esteem. But to be truly happy with ourselves and in life, we need to stop worrying about who others may think we are and start doing what we need to do to improve ourselves so that we can become the person we are trying to appear to be, if that is who we truly wish to be.

27

**The mind is everything.
What you think you become.**

(Buddha c. 563 BC – 483 BC)

What we think is what we perceive to be true or false about anyone and everything. This includes what we think and believe to be true or false about ourselves. What we think shapes our beliefs and values. It influences how we feel about ourselves and about people and things. It also determines how we define things and the standards and rules we attach to those things. All of this is a big part of who we are and who we become.

We are driven by what we think, that is, we do what we do based on what we think. If we think that we can achieve something, we are much more likely to take action and achieve it than if we were to think that our chances of achieving it are low or impossible.

Positive thinking will often lead to positive results and outcomes. If we think we will be happy and successful in life, we are likely to be happy and successful. If we expect the best, chances are we will get the best.

Positive thinking leads to a positive attitude. Attitude is a *way of thinking* reflected in the way we think about things. What we think about things affects the way we feel about those things. How we feel about those things influences how we respond to those things. How we respond will determine the results and outcomes we get. Some claim that 85-90% of what we get in life is the direct result of our attitude, our way of thinking.

What we think will have a direct effect on our self-esteem, self-confidence, attitude and personality, all of which will determine who we become, what we do in life, where, when and with whom. *Take good care of your mind*. Learn more, think and be positive and objective.

28

If evil be spoken of you and it be true, correct yourself, if it be a lie, laugh at it.

(Epictetus 55 – 135)

What others say about us is often merely their opinion of us. It's based on what they have heard or observed and how their brain has interpreted it all. Some people may say bad things about us simply to get us to *react*, to upset us or annoy us. Some may do it to control us, to push our buttons or pull our strings, to get us to do things they want us to do.

We need to listen objectively to what they say so that we can determine *whether* there is any truth to what has been said. We need to have an open mind, to listen to what they do say and to learn from it or discard it. We should look at it as an *opportunity* to have another look at ourselves and better ourselves for ourselves if what has been said is true. It may be an opportunity to fix or change things in ourselves that will make us better. If it isn't true, then we learn a little more about that person.

We can't control what others think of us or what they say about us. It can be difficult to simply ignore what others say, even if we know what they say is not true. But we can prevent what has been said from bothering us. What doesn't bother us, won't affect us.

It's important to understand and believe that it's not what someone says that affects us but rather it's our reaction, action or lack of action to what has been said. By improving our self-esteem, such things won't affect us. When we know who we really are and understand our emotions and have control of our emotions, what has been said won't get us to react. This enables us to *be objective* so that we can correct what needs correcting in ourselves (take action) and to ignore the rest.

29

The way to gain a good reputation is to endeavor to be what you desire to appear.

(Socrates 469 BC – 399 BC)

Our reputation is an opinion of us. It's who, what and how others believe we are. It's an image of us held by others based on their evaluation or the evaluation of us made by others. It may be they consider our character or personalty to be good or bad. Or it may be that they believe that we have a special skill or quality. It's what others think of us and it influences how they treat us.

It takes time, months, even years, to build a reputation, and one's reputation can be destroyed in days, even in seconds. Gaining a reputation can't be achieved simply by talking or telling others about ourselves. It can only be built by example – by action rather than words.

Actions that represent a good reputation include:

- Being polite and positive
- Acting with integrity, consistently
- Apologizing when wrong
- Being a good effective listener
- Doing what you say you will do
- Giving more than you promise and doing more than what is expected
- Not lying or cheating
- Being you, not your titles or position

Being and doing these things and more will enable us to gain a good reputation. A good reputation will follow us wherever we go in life. It will have a positive impact on what we do and get in our life, as it will attract the kind of people we want in our life.

30

We are free only insofar as we are in a position at every moment in our life to follow ourselves.

(Rudolf Steiner 1861 – 1925)

Freedom is the right to live as we wish. (Epictetus 55 – 135)
Freedom means that we can be who we are and wish to be. It also means that we can decide for ourselves what we want to do in and with our life and are able to do what we wish to do when we are ready to do it.

Freedom means the absence of fear, oppression, need, force or control. It means that we can think and believe what we wish to think and believe. It means that we can live our life based on our set of beliefs and values. It's about being able to make our own choices and decisions, and to do what we need to do when we decide to do it. It means that we are free to set our own goals and to do what we determine we need to do to achieve them.

Freedom enables us to do what we wish to do – freely. It means that we are in control of our time and have time to do the things we want and like to do. It means that we are physically, mentally, emotionally, and spiritually healthy. It also means that we are financially and emotionally independent and have a place we can and wish to call home.

To be free requires knowing who we want to be and what we want in life. It requires taking full responsibility for and maximum control of our life. It takes self-esteem (knowing we are worthy of being free) and self-confident (knowing we can be free.). To be free requires action. It requires taking care of our physical, mental, emotional and spiritual well-being. It requires getting and staying out of debt, and investing in our financial future. This enables us to follow ourselves.

31

As soon as you trust yourself, you will know how to live.

(Johann Wolfgang von Goethe 1749 – 1832)

When we trust ourselves, we will listen to our inner voice. This will enable us to discover who we *really* are. When we discover who that is and trust ourselves, we will want to discover and decide for ourselves who we wish to become. When we know who we wish to be, we can determine what we need to do so that we can be.

When we trust ourselves, we are able to discover our true strengths and any special talents or skills we have. We can also uncover any weaknesses or insecurities we might have. Knowing what they are can enable us to develop, improve, fix or overcome whatever they may be so that we can become who we truly wish to be.

When we discover who we truly wish to be and trust ourselves, we can determine the who, what, where and when we need to incorporate into our life. This enables us to determine the how, the things we need to do in order to incorporate those things into our life. When we have determined the how and we trust ourselves, we will want to take full responsibility for and maximum control of our life, as we will know how we need to live our life in order to get what we want in our life.

Trusting ourselves means that we are honest with ourselves, committed to ourselves and respect ourselves. It means that we have confidence in ourselves and that we value ourselves and can rely on ourselves to help ourselves to live life how we wish to live it. To do this, we need to have a healthy level of self-esteem and self-confidence. When we do, we will trust ourselves to determine for ourselves the criteria we use to determine how best to live our life – to live how we want to live.

32

Don't forget to love yourself.

(Soren Kierkegaard 1813 – 1855)

Loving yourself means looking out for No 1 – YOU. It means taking care of yourself and doing what's right and best *for you*. It means forgiving yourself and always improving yourself. Loving yourself is all about doing whatever you need to do so that you can be who you truly wish to be.

To be truly happy in life, we need to love ourselves. When we love ourselves, we feel good about ourselves. When we feel good about ourselves, we will believe and feel that we deserve to be who we really wish to be and to get and live the life we really want.

When we feel good about ourselves, we will depend on ourselves rather than needing to depend on others. When we depend on ourselves, we take control of ourselves and our life. When we take control of ourselves and our life, we can become who we truly wish to be and get and live the life we truly desire.

When we love ourselves, we respect ourselves and are comfortable with ourselves. This means that we don't need the approval or acceptance from others, as we will know the only person we need approval or acceptance from is ourselves. We will create our own set of values and standards and know that we're accountable to ourselves to meet them. This enables us to be ourselves.

Loving ourselves is about having a *healthy level* of self-esteem (not too much and not too little). It's about conquering any negative beliefs we may have about ourselves. It means that we don't put ourselves down but instead we take positive action to fix or improve things that we don't love about ourselves – so that we do.

PART 4
Happiness

Happiness is the meaning and the purpose of life, the whole aim and end of human existence.

(Aristotle 384 BC – 322 BC)

33

Happiness depends upon ourselves.

(Aristotle 384 BC – 322 BC)

Happiness lies within all of us. If we wish to be happy, it's up to us to see that we are. Happiness is subjective. It's what we believe it is, so only we are able to create it in our life. Our happiness depends upon ourselves to determine what happiness means to us and to ensure that we experience it in our life as often as we can.

For most of us, happiness means being who we truly wish to be doing what we truly wish to do in and with our life. It means being in good health and feeling well, at least most of the time. It means having close relationships and having a purpose and meaning in our life. And for most of us, it also means that life is fairly easy, favorable and free from difficult or troubling times or events.

Only we can do what needs to be done in order to become who we wish to be and to enable us to do what we really want to do in life – to be happy. Only we can know what truly makes us happy. Only we can put ourselves in places that, with people who, and do what enables us to experience happiness.

When we are healthy (physically, mentally, emotionally and spiritually), have a positive attitude, live in accordance with our own beliefs and values, achieve what we set out to achieve, live in a positive environment, have good relationships, maintain a good reputation, and meet our needs, we will experience happiness.

Only we can make all of this happen. We must depend on ourselves so that we can create and live a life filled with true happiness – to be healthy, to love, to be with people we enjoy being with, to do what we enjoy doing and to smile and laugh a lot.

34

We are more interested in making others believe we are happy than in trying to be happy ourselves.

(François de La Rochefoucauld 1613 – 1680)

Some of us may go through life trying to *convince* others that we are happy, even if we aren't. It may be that we:

- Talk about having a lot of money, as we may have been convinced that money means happiness.
- Buy expensive clothes, accessories or cars *to show* others that we have money, even if we don't.
- Buy things we don't need that media, marketing and advertising companies have convinced many people to believe makes people happy.
- Lie or exaggerate on social media sites about how great our life is, when in fact it may not be.
- Wear a fake smile, blurt out fake laughs or always talk about the past (a time when we were happy).

Trying to convince or fool others into believing that we are happy is a waste of time and energy, both of which could be used to be happy. Buying things that we don't need or truly want is money spent that could be spent on things that *would make us happy*, such as things that would enable us to improve ourselves. Doing things to *try to convince* others that we are happy, is time, energy and even money that could have been spent doing the things we truly enjoy doing, things that *make us happy*.

Be happy and stop trying to convince others to believe that you are happy. Discover what *you truly enjoy doing*. Discover the kinds of people you truly wish to spend your time with. Realize that although money can definitely make life easier, it can't buy happiness nor is it the indicator of happiness. Know what truly makes you happy, and do what you need to do to be happy.

35

Very little is needed to make a happy life; it's all within yourself, in your way of thinking.

(Marcus Aurelius 121 – 180)

The way we think (*our attitude*) determines who we are and whether we are truly happy in our life. The way we think is determined by how we view things, how we feel about things and how we act or respond to our views and feelings. Our beliefs, feelings and behavior (positive or negative) toward the things that we see and experience in our life are reflected in our attitude.

Getting what we really want in life, *making a happy life*, depends far more on our attitude than on our looks, family background, formal education, money, skills, knowledge or the people we know. This is because our *attitude* (our way of thinking) determines whether we have what it takes to make a happy life.

It's our attitude that enables us to forgive and forget, and to deal with or overcome our worries and fears. It's our attitude that will determine the choices and decisions we make and the results and outcomes we get. It's our attitude that will *give us the power* to set and achieve goals that will enable us to make a happy life.

It's not what has been said or done or what we saw or experienced that affects us (our happiness), but rather it's how *we allow* those things to affect us. Whether those things will affect us or how they will affect us depends on what we think and believe, how we feel, and how we respond to those thoughts, beliefs and feelings. In other words, it will depend on our attitude.

Being happy is a choice, and it's our attitude that will determine whether we choose to be happy. Very little is needed to make a happy life if we *have the right attitude*, a positive attitude. This will make all the difference.

36

Those who enjoy doing and enjoy what they have done are happy.

(Johann Wolfgang von Goethe 1749 – 1832)

Enjoyment is a feeling of pleasure one gets as a result of doing or experiencing something they like. It can also be a feeling of joyful satisfaction in doing something one feels good about. It could be the pleasure one gets when playing tennis or watching tennis. Or it might be the pleasure they get helping others. Getting pleasure from the things we do and experience makes us happy.

How we use our *life-time* will determine our happiness. The more pleasure and joyful satisfaction we get from our time, the happier we will be. When we enjoy the things we do and experience and have enjoyed what we have done and experienced, we will feel that our time has been well spent, and that makes us happy.

Pleasure and satisfaction are subjective and therefore it depends on what we like, that is, what gives us pleasure and joyful satisfaction. To be *truly happy* in life, we need to know what we like doing and experiencing and what we feel good about. This enables us to do more of the things that do give us pleasure and satisfaction.

When we know what we like, we can find and spend our time doing things with the kinds of people we enjoy being with. When we know what we like, we can find or create the kind of job doing things we enjoy doing and that provides us with the satisfaction we desire in a job. When we enjoy doing what we are doing, we get better at it, and this enables us to enjoy it even more. All of this makes us happy.

Happy people are more likely to be healthy, and being healthy enjoying doing what we do and having enjoyed what we have done is what being happy is about.

37

By desiring little, a poor man makes himself rich.

(Democritus 460 BC – 370 BC)

Looking beyond the basic needs we all require in order to live comfortably (fresh air, clean water, wholesome food, shelter, sleep, overall good health and healthy relationships), we don't need much to be rich.

To be rich means to *prosper*, to move forward in life. To prosper means to be happy and satisfied with who we are becoming and what we are doing and will do in our life. It means *being in control of our life*, which means:

- Being able to earn enough money so to have the things that enable us to feel good about ourselves.
- Having time to do the things we truly want to do, including to better ourselves.
- Having *some* desire but not desiring to have a lot.

Desire can make life more exciting. It can provide us with enthusiasm and energy. It can motivate and keep us determined to get what we desire. It can stimulate us to improve ourselves and our life, to become who we really want to be, earn enough money, and to live the life we really want to live. But at the same time, desire can take control of our life. Too much desire can drain us of our finances and time, can lead to mental or emotional problems, and even mess with our soul.

Desire for more is often a reaction to a feeling of unhappiness or a lack of satisfaction with oneself or life. Needs can be fulfilled but desires are often endless if we don't have control of ourselves. By limiting desire to that which will not take control of one's life, almost anyone can be rich – be truly happy and satisfied with who they are, who they are becoming, and with life.

38

Health is the greatest gift, contentment the greatest wealth, faithfulness the best relationship.

(Buddha c. 563 BC – 483 BC)

Being in good heath, being content with ourselves and our life, and having good relationships is the foundation of happiness.

Health is definitely the most important element of true happiness. Our overall health determines what we can and can't do in life. It determines whether we will have the energy to do the things we need to do in order to become who we wish to be and to create and live the life we desire to live. To be healthy is indeed a gift to be cherished and protected. Without it, we won't be happy.

For many people today, wealth only relates to money. But there is more to wealth than just money. Wealth really means abundance, a state of prosperity, to thrive. *Contentment* means to be generally satisfied with what we have, our state of prosperity. This includes meeting our basic needs. It also includes having control of ourselves and our life, having enough money to have the things that help us to be prosperous and happy (things like a good education, time to do the things we need to do and the time to do the things we enjoy doing), and being successful in what we do. Having all of this is what leads to contentment, to be truly wealthy.

To be happy, we need people in our life. We need to feel *closely connected* to others and to have social interactions. But we need the right kind of people and not too many people in our life to be happy. We need a close circle of friends who are faithful: loyal, honest, trusting and who truly wish for us to be who we really wish to be doing what we truly wish to do in our life. These make the best relationships and add to our happiness.

39

True happiness is to enjoy the present without anxious dependence upon the future.

(Lucius Annaeus Seneca 4 BC – 65 AD)

Buddhists practice living in the moment, experiencing life with all five (six) senses *as life is happening* around them. They are fully present, that is, aware of what is going on inside and outside of themselves at that moment. For most of us, doing the same would likely be difficult. But *to be truly happy*, we need to spend as much time as possible living in and enjoying the present.

Dependence upon the future can prevent us from being truly happy right now. Dependence can lead to anxiety and stress in the present. Anxiety and stress can take control of our life, which would prevent us from being happy. Being dependent upon the future for our happiness decreases our ability to truly enjoy the present and thus from experiencing true happiness.

By taking good care of the present we can reduce our anxiety or dependence on the future for our happiness. This means doing things *while living in the present* for our future. Doing so enables us to be happy now and can significantly increase our chances of being happy in the future. Things we can do is to:

- Take good care of our health and wealth today so that we'll also be healthy and wealthy tomorrow.
- Have a positive attitude, as a positive attitude is almost sure to mean a positive present and future.
- Stay out of debt, as debt means dependence on the future to get out of debt.
- Take the time and make the effort to choose the right friends and partner today. Being in the *wrong* relationships prevent us from enjoying life now.

40

Choose a job you love, and you will never have to work a day in your life.

(Confucius 551 BC – 479 BC)

Many of us work at a job 40-50 hours a week for 48-51 weeks a year from the age of 18 until we reach the age of 65. Considering that it takes us time to: get ready for work, get to and back from work, unwind after work, and to buy clothes for work, many of us spend about 21% of our life (122,640 hours) for work by the time we reach 65. That's 24 hours everyday for 14 years!

We are happier when we are doing what *we love doing*. When we are doing what we love to do, we are more motivated and more productive. We tend to strive to do the best we can. This leads us to get even better at what we love doing. Doing what we love to do is likely to put and keep us in a positive mood. It often leads us to feel more fulfilled and alive. All of this has a positive effect on our self-esteem, health, and our life.

When we know what we love doing, we can find a job (or *create* a way to apply what we love to do) that enables us to earn an income doing what we love to do. We can find a work environment that's right for us and work with people who also love to do what we love doing.

When we have a "job" doing what we truly love doing, work takes on a new meaning. It's not something that has to be done but rather something we enjoy doing. Time seems to fly by as we are doing what we truly enjoy doing, where and with people we enjoy being with. We benefit physically, mentally, emotionally, spiritually, and socially, and this makes us healthier and our life better and happier. Wouldn't you rather spend those 14 years (122,640 hours) doing something you truly love doing?

PART 5
Making Things Happen

People of accomplishment rarely sat back and let things happen to them. They went out and happened to things.

(Leonardo da Vinci 1452 – 1519)

41

It is not in the stars to hold our destiny but in ourselves.

(William Shakespeare c. 1564 – 1616)

What we do in and with our life is not predetermined, nor do the stars hold our destiny. Life *isn't about* waiting for life to happen, but rather it's a matter of deciding what we truly want in and from our life and taking full responsibility for and maximum control of our life. It's about taking the necessary action to create the life we want to live. It's this action that enables us to achieve all that we need to achieve in order to make our life happen the way we want our life to happen.

To fulfill our *destiny*, to live the life we are here to live, we need to rely on ourselves, not the stars. We need to have trust in ourselves so that we are able to determine for ourselves who we truly desire to become and what we truly desire to do in and with our life – our destiny.

Relying on and trusting ourselves enables us to make our own choices and decisions and to set our own goals. It also enables us to take whatever action is necessary in order to achieve those goals. When we rely on and trust ourselves, we decide how we act and react, and determine the right action to take, the action we need to take so that we can reach our full potential. We will also acknowledge that we alone are accountable to ourselves for the consequences of our actions. This triggers in us the *self-control* needed in order to have the patience, motivation, and determination required to live our destiny.

To believe that the stars hold our destiny is to enslave ourselves, as it stops us from listening to our inner self and following our heart and dreams. Knowing that our destiny lies within ourselves gives us the freedom to determine the course of our own life.

42

The secret of getting ahead is getting started.

(Mark Twain 1835 – 1910)

What we do today is what enables us to move forward in life; to get ahead in life, to become a better person, do something a little better, or have a little more than we had yesterday. If we do nothing, we are sure to get nothing. If we stand still, we are certain to go nowhere.

To become who we truly wish to be and to get and live the life we truly wish to live, we need to get started. To get started, we need to do something positive. We need to take action that will get us closer to becoming whoever and whatever that may be. In other words, we need to *take the initiative* to see to it that we get started – to do whatever we need to or should do, and continue to do so until we have made it to where we want to be.

As soon as we *get started*, we stop procrastination from taking control of our life. Once we have started, we are more likely to be determined to finish what we have started. When we're determined to finish what we have started, it will be much easier to keep going. Our determination will empower us to deal with and overcome any fears, obstacles or setbacks that might otherwise have led us to stop doing what we need to do in order to get ahead.

To get started, we need to have the motivation to start. This means we need to be inspired to get started. To get inspired, we need to *connect* pleasure or pain or benefits or rewards with doing what we need or want to start. We need to believe that we would *experience* that pleasure for doing or that pain for not doing what we need or should do, or that we would benefit or be rewarded for getting started. When we do, we can get ahead.

43

It does not matter how slowly you go as long as you do not stop.

(Confucius 551 BC – 479 BC)

Getting what we want in life, including becoming who we truly wish to become, requires desire, enthusiasm and perseverance. Once we decide what we desire in life, we need to be excited about getting it, do whatever it takes to get it and to keep at it until we do.

Aesop's fable *The Tortoise and the Hare* illustrates the value of moving forward regardless of how slowly we may progress toward reaching what we are aiming for. A lesson to be learned from this fable is – the speed at which we do things isn't what determines success but rather by doing things steadily and not stopping until they are done, we can achieve great success.

We cannot allow ourselves to be impatient, to believe that if we can't get it quickly it's not worth trying to get. Nor can we allow ourselves to put off doing things we should or need to do, convincing ourselves that we have plenty of time to do it later. Small and even slow steps forward, doing something, anything positive can move us closer to getting what we want in life. Taking time, but not too much time, and not stopping until we get what we are aiming for can enable us to become the person we dream of being and achieve amazing things.

Noting that for some things it does matter the speed at which we go. Some things require acting quickly, speed being of the essence, such as an opportunity that must be acted on immediately as the opportunity is available only to those who act swiftly. But generally, over a lifetime, by taking things one step at a time, even slowly, and persevering until we get it done, we are certain to get most of what we want in ourselves and in our life.

44

At the center of your being you have the answer; you know who you are and you know what you want.

(Lao Tzu 604 BC – 531 BC)

The saddest thing in life may be not knowing who we are and who and what we want to be. But it is possible to discover who and what that is. We can find the answers within ourselves if we take the time to find those answers – to discover ourselves.

Self-discovery is about searching deep inside ourselves to understand who we really are; what we truly think and believe, and how we truly feel about ourselves and things. It's about finding out what is truly important to us and discovering our true beliefs, values, needs, desires, likes, dislikes, goals and dreams.

Self-discovery is about searching deep inside ourselves to identify our uniqueness, abilities, attributes, attitudes, personality, strengths, weaknesses, limitations and any insecurities. It's about revealing to ourselves what we are passionate about and what we truly enjoy doing. Self-discovery is about looking beyond our subjective self (who we think or believe we are) and discovering our objective self (who we really are).

Self-discovery does take time and requires a genuine desire and a dedicated effort. Self-discovery requires asking ourselves a lot questions and being as objective as possible with each of our answers. These answers can reveal things that we didn't know about ourselves and things that we have tried to hide from ourselves.

Self-discovery alerts us to things we need to maintain, fix, improve, add or change in ourselves. It enables us to identify our potential, our purpose in life, and to figure out what's missing in our *self*. Knowing these things can enable us to make the best of ourselves.

45

First say to yourself what would you be; and then do what you have to do.

(Epictetus 55 – 135)

One of the toughest things in life may be deciding who we really want to be and what we really want to do in and with our life. By discovering who we are now, it's easier to decide who and what we truly wish to be. We can decide the who, what, where and when of our life, the things that would enable us to determine what we have to do to become who and do what we truly desire.

Once we have decided the who and what, and we know what we have to do, we need to:

- Take full responsibility for and maximum control of ourselves and our life.
- Have the right attitude – a positive attitude.
- Have the right mindset – believe in ourselves.
- Recognize any challenges or obstacles so that we can effectively deal with or overcome them.
- Fix, improve, eliminate or add things in ourselves or our life that need change. This means that we need to deal with or overcome any weaknesses, limitations or insecurities that we may have. It also means that we may need to develop, improve and utilize any strengths or special abilities we have.
- Make the right choices and decisions for us, those that will enable us to move forward.
- Set and achieve goals that enable us to become who and do what we really want to be and do in life.
- Do whatever it takes to make it all happen – take the right action so that we can make things happen the way we want those things to happen.

46

Do not let it be your aim to be something, but to be someone.

(Victor Hugo 1802 – 1885)

To be *something* means to do or become successful at something, such as being a bus driver, famous singer or surgeon. On the other hand, to be *someone* means to be, for instance, kind, honest, sincere, faithful, passionate, compassionate, generous, polite or respected.

We are not the job, career or profession we have, for instance, a clerk at the supermarket or a lawyer. We are not the academic, career, professional or corporate title or position we hold, such as professor or CEO. Nor are we the badge or uniform we wear, such as a police badge or a pilot's uniform. These are things we do, have or acquired in our life, but not who we are.

We are what we think, believe and value. We are how we feel about ourselves and the world around us. We are our attitude and personality, and all the definitions, rules and standards that we apply to people and things. These are the things that make us who we are.

We are all someone, and being someone we wish to be enables us to fulfill our life; to be proud, truly happy and satisfied with who we are. This has a *positive effect* on our self-esteem and self-confidence, both of which enable us to get more of what we really want in our life – to be happy with ourselves and the life we live.

Others can't take away who we are, but they can take away the things that make us something. We may lose our job. Eventually, we lose our position or fame. And one day we won't be doing what we did that made us something. People who are important to us might not care *what* we are or were, but it is and will be important to them *who* we are and were.

47

They are able because they feel they are able. They can do all because they think they can. They succeed because they believe they will.

(Virgil 70 BC – 19 BC)

To become who we truly wish to be and to create and live the life we truly wish to live, we must: feel that we are able (*self-confidence*), think we can (*positive attitude*) and believe that we will (*self-esteem*).

Self-confidence is what enables us to get things started and to get those things done. It's a feeling that we are capable of achieving what we set out to do. It's a feeling inside ourselves that we will succeed in what we do; that we will effectively choose, decide, plan, organize and take the action needed to become who we really want to be and to get what we really want in life.

What we do and don't do in life is based on what we think. If we think that we can (*positive*) do something, we can. If we think that we can't (*negative*), we can't. A positive attitude means positive thinking and having a positive mindset. Positive thinking is about concentrating on the positive elements, the cans, rather than the negative, the cannots. Having a positive mindset is about thinking that we can do something. Both can lead to positive action. Taking positive action is what gets positive results and outcomes, the things we need in order to get what we need and desire in our life.

Self-esteem is a reflection of how we feel about who we are. When we have a healthy level of self-esteem, we: feel good about ourselves, respect and value ourselves, feel we are worthy of having what we want in life, and will rely on and most importantly believe in ourselves.

Having a positive attitude and a healthy level of self-esteem and self-confidence gives us the best chance of getting what we need and truly desire in life.

48

The journey of a thousand miles begins with one step.

(Lao Tzu 604 BC – 531 BC)

To make things happen in our life the way we need or want things to happen, we need to do something to get things started. We need to take action regardless of how small that action may be. We need to take the first step, to do something, anything positive to make it happen.

If we don't start, we will never be able to become who we really wish to be or get to where we want to be. If we simply wait for things to happen, things are likely not to happen, at least not happen the way we really want them to happen. We may think and dream about who we wish to become. We may plan and set goals to do things in our life. But without taking action, taking the first step, those thoughts, dreams, plans and goals are likely to never be realized.

We need to start somewhere and start now. When we do, we are more likely to *follow through* with additional steps, eventually getting us what we want and where we wish to be. The first step may be to start believing that we are worthy of having and capable of getting what we want. The next step might be to identify and prepare for sacrifices we will need to make and challenges we may need to deal with so that we can keep doing what we need to do to get what we desire.

Recognize your starting point (the place where you are *now*) and the action to be taken (the action that will get you started) then take that first step. Do something positive *right now* toward becoming who and getting what you truly desire. That first step may be the hardest but without it, we go nowhere, we fail to truly experience and live life, our life journey never truly begins.

49

Great things are done by a series of small things brought together.

(Vincent Van Gogh 1853 – 1890)

Achieving great things in life never happens overnight. Great actors, movies, surgeons, drugs and inventions, for instance, are all the result of the small things done toward creating the greatness achieved in those things. This includes small things done toward getting things done that need to be done and the small things done to overcome things that could have otherwise prevented one from acquiring the greatness achieved.

Achieving great things in life often requires:

- A lot of time, effort, and determination.
- Overcoming or dealing with things that could get in the way of accomplishing great things.
- *Never believing* it's impossible to achieve and knowing when to adjust the steps required to achieve it.

We can achieve great things in our life by breaking up the things we need to do into a series of small projects or tasks that when brought together lead to our being able to do something great in and with our life. Breaking up these things into a series of smaller projects or tasks helps us to remain motivated and determined to do what needs to be done, as those things will be less intimidating – each project or task requiring less time and effort than it would take to accomplish the whole.

As accomplishing each of the smaller projects or tasks will require less time, we are more likely to see or experience some results and outcomes sooner. This will likely encourage us to make the time and to put in the effort to follow through with the next project or task in that series until we achieve the whole we truly desire.

50

Our life is what our thoughts make it.

(Marcus Aurelius 121 – 180)

It seems that our mind moves in the direction of our thoughts rather than away from them. If so, if we focus on the positive, our mind will move toward the positive. That is, if we think and expect the best, chances are we will get the best. If we have positive thoughts and expectations, chances are we are more likely to take on challenges and look for and act on opportunities, as we will think and expect that we will succeed. This helps us to create and get more of what we want in life.

Conversely, if we focus on the negative, our mind will move toward the negative. So if we were to think and expect the worst, chances are we would get the worst. If we had negative thoughts and expectations, chances are we would ignore challenges and opportunities, as we would think and expect that we wouldn't succeed. This ensures that we get less of what we want in life.

What we think will determine who we become. What we think about ourselves, people, places, events, concepts or things (*our attitude*) will determine what we do with and in our life. Positive thoughts and expectations lead to positive results and outcomes. The more positive thoughts and expectation we have, the more positive results and outcomes we are likely to get in life. This is the basic premise behind *positive thinking*.

What we consciously think about and focus on is our choice. We can consciously choose to think about and focus on the positive and create and nourish our mind with positive thoughts and images. Or we can choose to think about and focus on the negative and create negative thoughts and images, which can poison our mind.

51

What is not started today is never finished tomorrow.

(Johann Wolfgang von Goethe 1749 – 1832)

To become who we truly wish to be living the life we dream of living requires that we *start doing* today what needs to be done. The longer we wait to get started the longer it will take to finish. If we don't start, there will be nothing to finish.

Who we are and the life we live today is the result of all the things we started and finished and all the things we never started and thus never achieved. Who we are and the life we live tomorrow will *depend on* the things we start today and finish tomorrow.

To get started, we need to stop talking about it and start doing it. We need to overcome procrastination, which stops us from getting started. It's procrastination that stops us from fixing or changing things that need to be fixed or changed in ourselves or in our life (things that if fixed or changed would enable us to make our life happen the way we want it to happen). We need to control or eliminate whatever is stopping us from starting. It could be that we need to take control of an emotion or to eliminate something that is intimidating us, either of which can stop us from starting.

We also need to be proactive, to take the initiative to determine what we need to know and do in order to successfully start and finish what needs to get done. We need to exercise self-discipline. It's self-discipline that empowers us to do what we need, want or should do today – to do the things we may be putting off doing or don't want to do or feel like doing. It's self-discipline that propels us to start what needs to be started today and enables us to finish what we have started.

52

Fear defeats more people than any other one thing in the world.

(Ralph Waldo Emerson 1803 – 1882)

Fear can stop us from being who we are, as it can stop us from expressing ourselves – what we think, believe and feel. Fear can stop us from taking control of our life, as fear can mean that we choose: not to discover, not to try, not to experience, not to learn, and not to do what we should or need to do in order to fix the things in our life that aren't the way we want things to be.

Fear can stop us from taking risks, taking on challenges and taking advantage of opportunities. It's these risks, challenges and opportunities that *could* enable us to become who we really wish to be. It's these risks, challenges and opportunities that may enable us to achieve more and to get more in our life.

Fear can be stronger than our desire to become who we really want to be and to get and live the life we really want. It may be a fear of criticism or disapproval from others, making a mistake or making a wrong choice or decision, or simply fear of failure. It could be a fear of the discomfort or pain that we might need to endure in order to do or get what we want. Or it might be fear of the unknown or fear of change – not knowing the final results or outcomes of the actions we take or whether we will be able to handle change.

We need to overcome or take control of our fears. This enables us to take control of ourselves and our life, to make our own decisions and to do what we need or want to do (and not do things we don't want to do). To do that, we need to recognize and understand our fears. When we do, we can lessen, control and even eliminate many fears that may otherwise defeat us.

53

I am the master of my fate and the captain of my soul.

(William Henley 1849 – 1903)

People who truly excel in what they do in life, such as great athletes and truly happy people, take *full* responsibility for and *maximum* control of their life. They may have had trainers, advisers or supporters who helped them to maximize their true strengths and talents. But the person who excels makes the choice to do so. They are the one who decides to put in the time and effort that's required to get what they want. They are in control of their actions and reactions. They control what they do and how they do it. They take both the credit and the blame for what they do and what they get and don't get in life. They take action and get things done to make it all happen the way they want it to happen.

Taking responsibility for our life means taking control of our life, control the direction we take. Taking control means *choosing for ourselves* what we think and believe and how we feel, and controlling how we feel about the things that happen to us in our life. It means that we decide and live our life based on the definitions, rules, standards, beliefs and values that we believe are right and best for us, and we won't change them unless we determine that they need to be changed. It also means that we make our own choices and decisions and set our own goals, basing them on what we think, believe, feel and value. Taking control means that we determine who we become, what we do and get, and where we end up.

To become who we dream of being living the life we really want, we must be in control of ourselves and our life – we must be the master of our fate and the captain of our soul. This means that we cannot allow anyone or anything to take that control away from us.

54

When it's obvious that the goals cannot be reached, don't adjust the goals, adjust the action steps.

(Confucius 551 BC – 479 BC)

Goals are the blueprints to our happiness, instruments enabling us to become who and get what we want in life. When goals are combined with the right plans and strategies (action steps), we are able to make our dreams come true – to live a truly happy, fulfilling life.

Goals enable us to take control of our life. They give us the power to make things happen how we want things to happen in our life. They give us purpose and direction, something to aim for and work toward. They can put us in places where we wish to be, with people we wish to be with and in situations that can provide us with more happiness and satisfaction in our life. Goals, when achieved, enable us to become the best we can be and to do extraordinary things for ourselves and others.

To achieve our goals, we must be and remain focused, committed, disciplined, motivated, determined and put our plans and strategies into action. If doing so doesn't enable us to reach our goals, it doesn't mean that the goals aren't achievable or that they need to be adjusted or changed. What it does mean is that we may need to:

- Increase our focus, commitment, self-discipline, motivation, determination or knowledge or skills.
- Adjust or change our current plans or strategies.
- Break goals up into a series of smaller goals (*mini goals*) that when combined enables us to achieve the larger goal. And/or
- Change the time of day we work on a goal, a time *when we are most efficient* at doing what needs to be done to achieve that particular goal.

55

The wise make more opportunities than they find.

(Francis Bacon 1561 – 1626)

Opportunity means a chance, favorable circumstances, situation or occasion that could offer us something we need or want, or that we can use to help us to get what we desire. The *right opportunities* can enable us to make positive changes in ourselves and in our life.

We can create our own opportunities, and this means that our opportunities are infinite. Creating our own opportunities enables us to increase our overall well-being and quality of life. It enables us to fix or change things about ourselves that will enable us to feel good about who we are. It enables us to meet new people, those who are right for us. It can also enable us to open doors to a new and better job or career. In fact, creating our own opportunities can enable us to fix, improve, add or eliminate pretty much anything and everything in every aspect of our being and our life.

We can create our own opportunities by putting ourselves out there, being in places where the situation or circumstances are likely to offer what we desire. We can create our own opportunities by setting goals, as goals can provide us with endless opportunities to see and experience new things and places and to meet new people. New things, places and people open up even more opportunities that could get us what we desire.

Opportunity is about timing and timing is everything when it comes to opportunities. When we create our own opportunities, we can ensure that the timing will be right. In other words, we can be in right place at the right time when we are prepared to act so that we can get the most from those opportunities.

56

Small opportunities are often the beginning of great enterprises.

Demosthenes (384 BC – 322 BC)

The smallest opportunity can often be the beginning of bigger and better things in our life. Small steps forward from opportunities we act on can be progress toward achieving or obtaining what we desire. Such progress can boost our confidence. Self-confidence empowers us to act on even more opportunities. More opportunities can mean getting closer to and more of what we desire.

A small opportunity can often lead to bigger and better opportunities. Even if a small opportunity won't get us exactly what we need or desire, it may provide us with valuable lessons, knowledge and new skills, or maybe contacts that may be helpful to us in the future.

Often overlooked small opportunities is information, advice, suggestions or ideas offered by others. A single conversation with someone who has made, or has even failed to make, the same or similar changes in their life that we need or want to make in our life, could provide us with an opportunity to solve a problem or to avoid potential risks, challenges, obstacles or setbacks. That single conversation could provide us with information that could save us time or effort we would have needed to use in order to figure it out first hand. (Opportunity)

Getting what we really want in life is in part the result of a lot of small opportunities rather than a few large ones. Accomplishing difficult or large tasks, projects, goals and endeavors (*enterprises*) is often the end result of acting on what might have been seen as small or insignificant opportunities. Be it in our private, social or work life, acting on (the right) small opportunities can enable us to achieve great things in our life.

57

When one door closes another opens; but we often look so long and so regretfully upon the closed door that we do not see the one which has opened for us.

(Alexander Graham Bell 1847 – 1922)

Opportunities can help us to get what we need or want only when we can recognize or create and act on them *when the time is right*. Some opportunities might only be available for a few days, hours, minutes, or maybe just a few seconds. Unless we are able, willing and ready to act on them when the time is right, and know what we need to do when opportunities do knock, we may miss out on something that could have enabled us to make positive change in ourselves and in our life.

We can't allow ourselves to worry about, regret or focus our attention on opportunities we may have missed. To achieve and acquire the things we desire in our life, we need to forget about missed or lost opportunities. Instead, we need to use our time and energy to look for, recognize, find and create new opportunities that will enable us to achieve and acquire what we desire.

It's also important to realize that what we think about the concept of opportunity can influence and even determine the opportunities we do and don't see. Our upbringing, education, attitude, the people we know and those we spend time with, and where we live and work, all shape the way we perceive the notion of opportunity. For instance, if we're from an impoverished neighborhood, we may think or believe that we have little or no chance to attend college and therefore we may not recognize an opportunity that would enable us to do so.

We need to have the right attitude, take control of our thoughts, and believe that opportunities are all around us. Then we need to be on the look out for them and act on them so that they can help us to get what we want.

58

Actions speak louder than words.

John Pym (1584 – 1643)
(Abraham Lincoln 1809 – 1865)

What we do is far more important than merely speaking of what we will do, have done or promise to do. Those who don't backup what they say with action or proof are often seen as being a hypocrite, big mouth, bragger or liar, someone who doesn't, didn't, can't, and likely won't do what they say. As they continue to fail to do so, they lose credibility and damage their reputation.

The expressions *Talk the Talk Walk the Walk* and *Talk is Cheap* also refer to the notion that what someone does is far more important than what someone says. What someone says and does is a great determinant of one's character. If someone says something but acts contrary to what they did say, they may appear to others to be someone who cannot be relied upon or trusted.

Our beliefs and values are a big part of who we are. We are often judged by others based on those beliefs and values. Only speaking of rather than living our life by those beliefs and values is sure to affect that judgment. Doing rather than saying provides visual confirmation. What we do shows our beliefs, values, intentions and feelings. Seeing is believing.

For instance, if we tell our partner that we will change, we need to take action to change, and change – not say that we will change. Or if we tell others that we're trustworthy, we need to be honest – not lie or deceive.

When we take action, not only do we get things done, we also strengthen our character and reputation. In return, we gain respect from others. Respect from others makes us feel better about who we are, and this makes our life happier.

59

Perceive that which cannot be seen with the eye.

(Miyamoto Musashi 1584 – 1645)

Our eyes merely see reflected light. For us to *see* things, our brain needs to make assumptions about what it sees. These assumptions are based on our perception of those things. It's our subjective evaluation and interpretation of those things (*perception*) that makes meaning of them – determines what we see.

Our perception is our reality, what things mean to us. It's what we think is true, real and important. It's what we believe about ourselves, and what we believe other people think and feel about us. Our perception influences things like our personality, behavior, emotions and attitude. It influences what we like and dislike and impacts the choices and decisions we make. It determines the goals we set and importantly whether or not we will achieve those goals. All of this determines who we are today, and greatly influences and may likely determine who we will become, what we do, and what we get in life tomorrow.

But, what is real in the universe is objective. That is, it's not what we might think or believe something is, but rather it's what it actually is. This means that we need to be as objective as possible before believing what we see and before doing the things we do in life. We also need to be as objective as possible when making judgments, choices and decisions, and setting goals.

To get what we want in life and to be happy in life, we need to understand the difference between *subjective* and *objective*. This enables us to look beyond ordinary sight (perception) so that we are able to see and understand things for what and how they really are.

60

There is nothing impossible to those who will try.

(Alexander the Great 356 BC – 323 BC)

The impossible is always (almost always) possible. Just think of the impossibles Oprah Winfrey has achieved. Born in impoverished rural Mississippi to an unwed teenage mother, suffering years of abuse and hardship, Oprah has become one of the most influential women in the world. Consider J.K. Rowling, who was a single mother living off welfare. Her Harry Potter novels has led to the creation of a multi-billion dollar empire.

To achieve the impossible, we need to:

- Take 100% responsibility for and maximum control of ourselves and our life.
- Have the right attitude. It's our attitude that will determine whether we will find or create a way to achieve the impossible. We must have a positive attitude and mindset.
- Believe in ourselves. To do the impossible, we need to trust and believe that we can and will take the right action needed to accomplish what we want. When we believe that we can, we can, but if we believe that we can't, we simply can't and won't.
- Set and achieve goals. Goals are the beginning to achieving and acquiring what we and others may have thought impossible.
- Remain persistently motivated and determined to do *whatever* we need to do to achieve what we set out to achieve. This enables us to effectively deal with or overcome challenges, obstacles, setbacks, difficulties, fear, pain, or opposition from others that we might face or experience along the way to achieving the impossible.

61

That some achieve great success is proof to all that others can achieve it as well.

(Benjamin Franklin 1706 – 1790)

The 1639 idiom, *Seeing is believing*, is as true today as it was more than 380 years ago when it comes to achievement. To see others achieve great success is *proof* that it can be done and this can provide us with the motivation we need to set out to do and achieve the same, or more.

To achieve great success ourselves, we need to:

- Know exactly what we want to achieve. This will enable us to determine what we will need to do in order to achieve it. But be discerningly realistic.
- Wholeheartedly believe that we will succeed.
- Have the *right* attitude and mindset. This includes being motivated, determined and committed.
- Have the right level of self-esteem and self-confidence. A lot but never too much.
- Recognize, find and create opportunities that will help us get what we are aiming to achieve.
- Learn from our mistakes and those of who have succeeded. We must *learn from* failure or mistakes and not allow either to kill our enthusiasm.
- Know what we must know, have or acquire whatever it is, then put it into action.
- Know what could stop us from succeeding so that we can do something so that it doesn't stop us.
- Take responsibility for and control of our life. This means *no excuses, blame, fear or jealousy of others.*
- Make the right choices and decisions. Set the right goals with the right plans and strategies. Take the right action and don't stop until we succeed.

PART 6
Old Sayings

Dig the well before you are thirsty.

(Chinese Proverb)

62

Even monkeys fall from trees.

(Japanese Proverb)

We all make mistakes. Maybe we over estimated our abilities, knowledge or skills, which led to our making a mistake. Or it might be that we made a bad choice, judgment or decision and that led to our making the mistake. Making mistakes is a part of life and should be a part of learning about life.

If falling from the tree does not kill the monkey, the monkey will simply shake it off and climb up the tree yet again and do what monkeys do. Maybe a different tree at a different time, but the monkey will climb yet again. Monkeys don't make excuses or look for others to blame when they fall. Neither should we.

Mistakes and failure can bruise our self-esteem and self-confidence. However, to *move forward*, we need to admit to ourselves if we make a mistake or fail and learn from it. By identifying the reasons for our mistakes and failures, we can maintain control of our future, as doing so will enable us to avoid making the same mistakes or failing in the future. Knowing the why enables us to do things differently the next time so our past mistakes don't become a part of our future. It may even help us to deal with and overcome our mistakes and failures.

When we recognize our mistakes (our wrong choices, judgments, decisions, actions or reactions) and learn from those mistakes, we can move forward. We can find and create better choices, make better judgments and better decisions, take better action and avoid reacting – today and in the future. This will give us the power to get better results and outcomes; results and outcomes that will get us what we truly want in our life.

63

He who asks is a fool for five minutes, but he who does not ask remains a fool forever.

(Chinese Proverb)

Many of us were afraid to ask questions in elementary and middle school. We likely thought that raising our hand was sure to make us look stupid in the eyes of our classmates. It only got worse in high school, as our peers, we thought, would judge us, think that we were an idiot for asking. (You can bet many wished someone would ask so that they too would get the answer.) What we may not have realized was that not asking questions was stupid and only an idiot wouldn't ask.

Getting what we really desire in life requires that we have the information and skills needed to get it. To get the life we really want, we need answers. Asking is an opportunity to learn something we may not know or to correct or improve what we think we know. *Knowledge* is fundamental to our becoming who we truly wish to be and doing what we really want to do in and with our life. Asking enables us to get the answers we need in order to gain that knowledge.

Ask and consider what others have to say. It might help us to get what we truly wish in life, and possibly get it easier and quicker. Asking could save us time and effort having to experience things for ourselves – to learn about something firsthand. It could be that we might not have thought about, heard before or haven't experienced or seen some of the things someone else has. Those things just might be what we need to know to help us to solve a problem or to do something we couldn't do before. If we ask and listen with an open mind and objectively think about what they say, we may find that what others say can help us to create and live the life we truly desire.

64

Don't expect anything from anyone [other than yourself]. You won't be disappointed when they don't do as you expected.

(Old Saying)

Our expectations are based on our set of definitions, rules and standards, the set that we have (hopefully) determined for ourselves. Some of our definitions, rules and standards are certain to be *different from* the people we work with and spend our time with. For instance, what we might believe to be right behavior, based on our definitions, rules and standards, might not be the way other people see or define it. Or it could be that the rules and standards they have attached are different.

We can't expect others to know what we are thinking or what we want. We can't expect them to always agree with what we think or believe or to understand how we feel. And we can't expect them to do what we want them to do or to do it the way we expect them to. Even if we were to tell others our set of definitions, rules and standards, chances are they might interpret them differently than we do. They may simply think, believe, feel, see and do things differently.

People will not always meet our expectations of them. When others don't meet our expectations, it can hurt. We might feel betrayed, let down, disappointed, sad, bad, mad or even unloved. But we can't allow ourselves to feel that way when they don't meet our expectations. But we can choose to expect nothing from others. By doing so, if they don't do what we expect it won't hurt.

We should, however, always have high expectations of ourselves. Never allow yourself or anyone to convince you to expect little or nothing from yourself or in your life. When we meet our own high expectations, we are certain to be happier with ourselves and get more in life.

65

Spilled water will not return to the bowl.

(Japanese Proverb)

Once something has been done, it can't be undone. It has happened, it is a part of the past. We might be able to do something to change the *consequences* of what has been done, but things will never be the same. Cheating on your partner, for instance, can't be undone. Even if you were to continually apologize and show true regret, if you did it, you did it. What you did can't be undone. This also applies to time. Time spent is gone forever. We can't be credited with that time to use that time at another time. Once gone it's gone.

We need to think before we act or react so that we don't do something that we later wish we hadn't done. This includes: doing, not doing, saying or not saying something. We also need to know what we truly desire to achieve and acquire in our life so that we don't waste time (our *life-time*) doing things that won't get us closer to getting what we truly desire.

We need to do whatever we can do to do things right the first time, and to not do the wrong things. Doing things that we wish we hadn't done can often lead to results, outcomes or consequences that can't be undone. It can lead to us regretting the past for what we've done. This can keep us focused on the negative and have a negative effect on our attitude and our health. It could even destroy our health, relationships and our life.

To live the life we really want, we need to admit to our mistakes, apologize when we are wrong, fix what we can, drop what we can't, learn and move on. Endeavor to do the right thing. Life is too short to spend it worrying, regretting or dealing with things we can't undo.

66

To know the road ahead, ask those returning.

(Chinese Proverb)

We can *learn* from the experience of others. Asking those who have experienced things we are thinking of doing or aiming to achieve in life can save us time, energy, money, even pain having to experience it ourselves.

What they have seen, experienced and learned may be what we need to know to help us to get what we want in our life. Their thoughts, advice or suggestions might provide us with the knowledge we need to enable us to avoid disappointment or pain, or spending our time, energy and even money learning for ourselves.

It could be that they know the things to look out for and when to look for those things, like risks, obstacles, challenges or problems that would otherwise slow us down or stop us from getting what we want. Or it may be that they know the dangers or pain that is involved in doing or trying to achieve what we are thinking of doing or achieving. Knowing these things could better prepare us in the event that we do encounter the same or similar difficulties and to avoid the dangers or pain.

They may know the advantages, pleasures, benefits and rewards of doing or achieving the things we're thinking of doing or achieving. They may also know how to do and achieve those things more effectively and quicker.

We need to ask, think about and decide for ourselves if their thoughts, advice or suggestions could help us to get closer to getting and living the life we really want. It might be things about marriage or living with someone, having a child, or a career or profession that could help us to make the *right decisions for us*. Getting these things right will make a huge difference in our life.

67

Teachers open the door, but you must enter by yourself.

(Chinese Proverb)

Teachers can teach us but only we can learn what they teach. They can't force us to listen or learn No one can make us learn but ourselves. It is up to us to actually do or don't do whatever we have been taught, to think about and apply what is being taught. This applies to everything we are taught. For instance:

- Our mother told us not to touch a hot stove, but for some of us, we just couldn't resist. But once we did touch it, it became clear, we learned that it is not to be touched.

- Maybe our father, mother, brother or sister taught us the tricks and techniques to riding a bicycle. But we were the one who got on, tried to balance and pushed the pedals in order to go forward.

- In a foreign language class, the teacher can guide us, teach us the rules of grammar, etc., but only we can put what we are taught into action, to master that language, to speak and write in that language. There are always some students who excel while others don't. Same teacher same material but it's how the student applies what they are taught.

Teachers are opportunities to learn and they are everywhere. We simply need to recognize them, learn from them, and importantly apply what we learn. There are teachers in our relationships (our parents, partner and friends). There are teachers at work (our boss and co-workers). There are even teachers to teach us about new places, cultures and people (travel). Doors are opened all around us. We just need to *act* (enter) to learn. What we learn can help us to get what we truly want in life.

68

Believe nothing you hear and only half of what you see.

(Old Saying)

What we believe influences who we are, who we will become and what we do and get in our life. What we believe influences and shapes our attitudes about: sex, marriage, affairs, money, alcohol, drugs, crime, status, success, material things, people of different cultures, colors and religions, and our view on our role in society. All of this influences and even determines the choices, judgments, decisions and actions we make and take in our life.

We can be influenced by what teachers, mentors, people we respect and admire, and even celebrities say or do. We are often influenced by what society and our peers say and do. The media often provides us with its own perceptions of who or what people and things are, how and what these people and things are supposed to be and whether they are important or acceptable. And the real masters of persuasion, marketing and advertising people, have for years used various methods and techniques to *push the right buttons* and *pull the right strings* to get us to believe what they want us to believe.

Sometimes there's more to what we hear and see. Sometimes what we hear and see is incomplete, inaccurate or simply isn't true. And sometimes it just isn't right *for us*.

To be who we truly wish to be living our life the way we truly wish to live it, we cannot believe everything we hear or see. If we do, we will be misguided – taken further away from rather than getting closer to what we truly desire. We need to listen to and observe *carefully and objectively* what we hear and see, and then make our own rational determination as to what we believe.

69

Don't stand by the water and long for fish; go home and weave a net.

(Chinese Proverb)

We can't simply sit around *waiting* for things to happen the way we want things to happen. We cannot expect other people to make the things we need or want to happen. And we definitely can't rely on others to make things happen for us the way we need or want things to happen in our life.

For things to happen the way we need or want things to happen in our life, we need to take action. We need to do something and need to do it ourselves. We need to be proactive.

Being proactive means that we anticipate, change and initiate. It means that we look ahead, we consider what *may* happen. It could mean that we may need to adjust or change some of our definitions, rules or standards, or some of our beliefs or values. It could mean that we may need to change our attitude so that we have the right attitude needed in order to get what we desire. Being proactive means that we make our own choices and decisions, find and create our own opportunities and set our own goals. And most importantly, it means that rather than simply wishing, wanting or dreaming of having or doing something (longing for) – *we take action*. We do whatever we need to do in order to make the things that we can control happen the way we want them to happen.

Being proactive (anticipating, changing and initiating) gives us the best chance of getting what we truly desire in life. Being and remaining proactive throughout our life enables us to succeed and prosper, and to become the best that we can be.

70

Fall seven times and stand up eight.

(Japanese Proverb)

Those who become who and get what they really want in life are those who don't allow the things that knock them down to keep them down. When knocked down, they do something positive to enable them to get back up, to keep moving forward. They don't complain or worry about the things that had knocked them down. They don't make excuses or look for someone to blame. They simply dust themselves off and learn from what had knocked them down. They adjust or use a new approach or method to get the results and outcomes they want. They simply do it again a little differently than the way they did it before and keep getting up until they get what they need and desire.

We all get knocked down. When life knocks us down, we need to get right back up. If we stay down, we are giving up on ourselves and our life. By staying down, we are willing to accept less of ourselves and less from our life. If we fail to get back up, we are allowing other people, obstacles, setbacks, mistakes or past failures to stop us from getting and living the life we could have made happen, a life that's perfect for us.

To create and live a life that's perfect for us, we need to know what that is. We need to be healthy and to have a *healthy level* of self-esteem and self-confidence. We need to take full responsibility for and maximum control of our life. We *must have* the right attitude and mindset. We need to be proactive, enthusiastic and persistent. We need to do whatever needs to be done, which includes getting up each time we are knocked down. We need to continue to move forward so that we *can make our life happen the way we truly want it to happen*.

Biographies for these 70 Timeless Quotes and Sayings

Abraham Lincoln (1809 – 1865) was the 16th President of the United States. Lincoln led the then United States through the American Civil War. In doing so, he preserved the Union (the national government, the then 23 free states and five border states that supported the government), strengthened the federal government and abolished slavery. Mainly self-educated, he became a lawyer, political orator and insightful politician promoting the modernization of the economy via banks, tariffs and railroads. He is considered to be one of the three greatest US. Presidents to this day.

Aesop (621 BC – c. 564 BC) was a Greek fabulist, story teller, whose existence remains uncertain. He has been credited with numerous fables; moral and ethical teachings through stories, often with animals as main characters. These are collectively known as *Aesop's Fables*, first printed in English in 1484. Whether Aesop actually existed is irrelevant, as he has fondly lived in the hearts of the hundreds of millions of people who grew up reading and listening to his stories.

Alexander Graham Bell (1847 – 1922) was a scientist, inventor, engineer and innovator who, in 1876, was awarded the first US. patent for the telephone. He left high school at the age of 15, but later attended University of Edinburgh and was later accepted at the University of London. Although he did not complete university in his youth, he received a number of honorary degrees from academic institutions, including eight honorary Doctorate of Laws, two Ph.D.s and an M.D. Alexander Graham Bell held 18 patents in his name and is credited with having performed innovative work in optical telecommunications, hydrofoils and aeronautics.

Alexander the Great (356 BC – 323 BC) was a King of the Ancient Greek kingdom of Macedon. At the age of twenty, he succeeded the throne from his father. By the age of thirty, he had created an empire stretching from Greece to northwestern India. For a brief period of time, his empire was the most powerful State in the world. As a consequence of his military conquests, he greatly increased trade between East and West and founded many cities, some of which he named after himself. He has been ranked one of the most influential people in history. Never having lost a battle, military schools around the world continue to study and teach his military tactics.

Aristotle (384 BC – 322 BC) was a Greek philosopher and scientist, and student of Plato. He tutored the then 13-year old Alexander the Great, for two or three years. He wrote, researched, taught, influenced and contributed to a wide range of disciplines, including medicine, philosophy, logic, ethics, morals, metaphysics, politics, economics, psychology, and religion. Aristotle has been referred to as *the greatest philosopher in history* (Ayn Rand), and modern philosopher Bryan Magee argues that *it is doubtful whether any human being has ever known as much as he* [Aristotle] *did*. Aristotle wrote an estimated 200 works, of which only 31 remain. It is claimed that Aristotle's writings were the foundation of the first comprehensive system of Western philosophy.

Benjamin Franklin (1706 – 1790) was, among many things, a leading author, printer, diplomat, political theorist, civic activist, statesman, politician, scientist, and inventor. As an inventor, he's best known for the lightning rod/*kite experiment* and the invention of bifocals. His formal schooling ended when he was ten. He wrote several works. Among the best known is *Poor Richard's Almanack*, a yearly almanac that contained the calendar, weather, poems, sayings, and astronomical and astrological information. It was published for 25 years under the pseudonym of Richard Saunders. Although never serving as U.S. President, he is considered to be one of the *Founding Fathers of the United States of America*, signing both the U.S. Declaration of Independence and Constitution.

Buddha (c. 563 BC – 483 BC) was an ascetic (one who leads a simple life, abstaining from normal pleasures of life, such as material possessions, often dedicating their life to pursuit of contemplative ideals) and sage (one who has attained the wisdom which a philosopher seeks). Born in what is now Nepal, he lived and taught mostly in the eastern part of India. His teachings are the foundation of Buddhism, which spread around the world and has become one of the world's major religions.

Confucius (551 BC – 479 BC) was a Chinese teacher, politician and philosopher. He advocated strong family loyalty, ancestor worship and respect of one's elders, and embraced the law of reciprocity, the principle *Do not do to others what you do not want done to yourself.* (Principle shared with nearly every religion.) His teachings emphasized education and study, the importance of compassion or loving others, and the view that rulers should be self-disciplined and govern their subjects by their own example. After his death, Confucius' teachings were converted by his disciples and followers into a set of rules and practices, later compiled into a work called *Analects*. (A collection of sayings and ideas attributed to Confucius.) These rules and practices became official imperial philosophy in China, and were required reading for civil service exams in 140 BC, continuing until the end of the 19th century.

Democritus (460 BC – 370 BC) was a scientist, a pioneer of mathematics and geometry, and a Greek philosopher. He is regarded by many to be *the father of modern science*, primarily remembered for his formulation of an atomic theory of the universe. Other than fragments from his works, none of his writings have survived. For Democritus, knowledge of the truth is difficult since for most people, *truth* is their perception of the truth, which is subjective and thus not necessarily the truth.

Demosthenes (384 BC – 322 BC) was a Greek statesman, legal writer and advocate, and politician. He was recognized as *the perfect orator who lacked nothing* and as one of the ten greatest orators and speechwriters of the Classical Era (5th – 4th century BC). His writing and orator skills enabled him to manage any kind of court case, adapting his skills to almost any kind of situation or client. He played a major role in opposing the then new King of Macedonia, Alexander the Great. His techniques, ideas and principles still influence politicians, lawyers, and political movements today.

Epictetus (55 – 135) was a philosopher. Spending his youth as a slave, his owner permitted him to study philosophy. After having obtained his freedom, he taught philosophy in Rome and then in Greece. He taught that philosophy is a way of life, and that each of us is responsible for our own actions. His students included Marcus Aurelius (the second century Roman emperor).

Euripides (480 BC – 406 BC) was a tragedian playwright (a writer of tragedies) and poet of classical Athens (508–322 BC). His theatrical *innovations* included introducing intrigue into his plays, with plots of revenge, insanity and suffering. His focus was on his characters' inner lives and motives, their passions and intense emotions, and being sympathetic towards victims of society, including women. His style is considered to have had a major influence on the creation of Greek New Comedy (320 BC to about 260 BC) offering a mildly satiric view of contemporary Athenian society. It also has had a profound influenced on modern writers today, such as John Milton and T.S. Eliot.

Francis Bacon (1561 – 1626) was an English statesman, officer of the court, scientist, philosopher and author. He has been called the father of *empiricism* (basing ideas and theories on testing and experience). Best known for the idea that scientific knowledge can be based only upon inductive observation and experimentation. This continues to be the way scientific research is conducted today.

François de La Rochefoucauld (1613 – 1680) was a member of the French governing establishment, soldier, and author. His works consists of *Memoirs*, *Maxims*, and his letters. In *Maxims*, he reflects on people's conduct and motives (human ethics and morals). His works influenced many, such as 19th century German philosopher Friedrich Nietzsche.

Henry David Thoreau (1817 – 1862) was an American poet, essayist, historian, and philosopher. Likely best remembered for his philosophical and naturalist writings and best known for his book *Walden*, a look at simple living in nature. His essay *Resistance to Civil Government* (a.k.a. *Civil Disobedience*), a call for improving rather than abolishing government by way of nonviolent resistance, has had a major impact on civil rights movement leaders, such as Gandhi and Martin Luther King, Jr.

Horace (65 BC – 8 BC) was a Roman lyric poet, satirist and critic. He's best known today for his work *Odes* (a collection of Latin lyric poems in four books), which praises common events and ordinary thoughts and sentiments of social life of Rome in the age of Augustus (63 BC – 14 AD). The most frequent themes in *Odes* are love, pleasures of friendship, morality, and a simple life. His works influenced later poets, playwrights, and writers, including Dante, Voltaire, Goethe, and Frost.

Johann Wolfgang von Goethe (1749 – 1832) was a German lawyer, editor, philosopher, scientist, playwright, and poet. He has been regarded as the genius of modern German literature. His works cover the fields of poetry, literature, philosophy, and science. His first widely-read novel, *The*

Sorrows of Young Werther, became an international success. Napoleon Bonaparte called the novel one of the greatest works of European literature. Goethe's famous work, the poem-as-play, *Faust* was adapted into a grand opera, which is still performed today worldwide. He wrote volumes of poetry, essays, criticism, and scientific works on evolution and linguistics. Goethe's influence was immense.

John Pym (1584 – 1643) was an English lawyer, prominent member of the English Parliament, and critic of King James I and later King Charles I. A political activist and leader of the political opposition to the King and his supporters, Pym's aim was to find what he considered to be the right balance between the power of the Crown (King or Queen) and that of Parliament.

Lao Tzu (604 BC – 531 BC) was a Chinese philosopher and writer. He has been traditionally regarded as the author of the *Tao Te Ching* and founder of philosophical Taoism. His works have influenced political theorists and libertarians (e.g., anti-authoritarian movements).

Leonardo da Vinci (1452 – 1519) was a polymath (a person whose expertise covers a number of different fields). He is widely regarded as one of the greatest painters of all time. His *Mona Lisa* and *The Last Supper* are likely his most famous paintings. He was also an inventor, writer, sculptor, scientist, engineer, and mathematician. Undoubtedly, he was one of the most diversely talented people ever to have lived.

Lucius Annaeus Seneca (4 BC – 65 AD) was a philosopher, statesman, and dramatist. He was a teacher and adviser to the Roman emperor Nero. Later he was forced to commit suicide for alleged involvement in a conspiracy to assassinate Nero. Regarded as the source and inspiration for *Revenge Tragedy*, Seneca influenced playwrights such as Shakespeare.

Marcus Aurelius (121 – 180) was Roman Emperor from 161 to 180 and a philosopher and writer. He wrote *Meditations of Marcus Aurelius* (title added after his death), which today is considered to be a major source of understanding of ancient Stoic philosophy. During his life, he acquired the reputation of a *philosopher king*, a title that remained after his death. He has been portrayed in the movies, *The Fall of the Roman Empire* and in *Gladiator*.

Mark Twain (1835 – 1910), whose real name was Samuel Clemens, was a writer, entrepreneur, publisher, and adamant supporter of the abolition of slavery and freeing of slaves. Most famous for his novels, *The Adventures of Tom Sawyer* and *Adventures of Huckleberry Finn*, Twain is one of few authors whose works have been published as new best-selling books in all three of the past three centuries, his last in 2010.

Michelangelo (1475 – 1564) was a sculptor, painter, architect, poet, and engineer. He is considered to be the greatest living artist during his lifetime. He has also been described as one of the greatest artists of all times. His best-known works are likely that of the *Statue of David* and his paintings scenes in the Sistine Chapel in Rome, including *The Creation of Adam* and *The Last Judgment*. His influence on the development of Western art is unparalleled.

Miyamoto Musashi (1584 – 1645) was an expert Japanese swordsman and rōnin (a samurai without a master). He was also a talented artist, sculptor, and calligrapher. He gained fame through stories of his skill and unique double bladed swordsmanship. He held an undefeated record of 60 duels. He founded the Niten-ryū style of swordsmanship, a style in which one uses both a large sword and a smaller sword at the same time. Before his death (by natural causes), he wrote a book on strategy, tactics, and philosophy, entitled *The Book of Five Rings*, which is still read today.

Plutarch (46 – 120) was a Greek historian, biographer, and essayist. His writings and lectures led to him to become a celebrity in the Roman empire. His best-known work is his *Parallel Lives*, a series of biographies of famous Greeks and Romans, organized in pairs to set out their common moral virtues and vices. His works had an enormous influence on English and French literature, including that of Shakespeare, Francis Bacon, and Ralph Waldo Emerson.

Ralph Waldo Emerson (1803 – 1882) was an essayist, lecturer, and poet. He wrote on a variety of subjects; developing ideas on individuality, freedom, and people's ability to acquire or achieve almost anything. One of his well-known essays is entitled, *Self-Reliance*. His works not only influenced those in his day, like Walt Whitman and Henry David Thoreau, they continue to influence philosophers and writers throughout the world today.

Rudolf Steiner (1861 – 1925) was an Austrian philosopher, writer, painter, and architect. His ideas led to the creation of a system of agriculture that contributed to the development of today's organic farming. Working with doctors, his ideas led to the development of a range of medications and therapies. Some of his paintings and drawings have influenced modern artists, and two of his building designs have been widely recognized as masterpieces of modern architecture.

Socrates (469 BC – 399 BC) was a philosopher recognized as one of the founders of Western philosophy. Renowned for his contribution to the field of ethics, for Socrates, the best way for people to live is to focus on the pursuit of *virtue*; moral excellence, good, and justice, rather than, for instance, on material things. He linked virtue with joy and taught that if people know what is right, they will naturally do what is good. His most valuable contribution to Western thought may be his *dialectic method of inquiry*, the Socratic method.

Soren Kierkegaard (1813 – 1855) was a philosopher, social critic, poet, theologian, and writer. Much of his philosophical work related to the thought of how people live as a single individual, emphasizing the importance of personal choice and commitment. His works have had a major influence on psychology and 20th-century literature, such as the works of American poet and novelist John Updike.

Victor Hugo (1802 – 1885) was a poet, novelist, and dramatist. He is considered to be one of the greatest and best-known French writers. His works include the novels, *Les Misérables* and *The Hunchback of Notre-Dame*. *Les Misérables*, which was later edited into a theatrical musical and a film, remains one of the best-known works of 19th century literature.

Vincent Van Gogh (1853 – 1890) was a painter. Although considered a lunatic and a failure in his lifetime, today, he is considered to be the second greatest Dutch painter ever (after Rembrandt). He has created some of the most *powerful* art ever created. Today, his paintings sell for tens of millions of dollars, and a few for more than hundred million dollars.

Virgil (70 BC – 19 BC) was one of ancient Rome's greatest poets. His works have had a major influence on Western literature. The *Aeneid* (although unfinished at his death) is considered to be his finest work. (The *Aeneid* is a story about Aeneas, the mythical Trojan hero who, after the fall of Troy, traveled to Italy to battle the Latins, eventually becoming the mythical root of Roman ancestry.) Virgil's *Aeneid*, *Eclogues* and *Georgics* were all standard texts in school curricula in ancient Rome.

William Henley (1849 – 1903) was an English poet, critic, and editor. He was recognized as having a major influence on the literary culture during the late Victorian era. His poem *Invictus*, written in 1875, is likely his best remembered work.

William Shakespeare (c. 1564 – 1616) was an English poet, playwright, and actor. He has been regarded as the greatest writer in the English language. Some of his works include *Hamlet*, *Macbeth*, *Romeo and Juliet*, *The Merchant of Venice*, and *A Midsummer Night's Dream*. His plays have been translated into every major language and are performed more often than the works of any other playwright.

More from Simple Logic Publications
Available on Amazon and other online book sellers' websites.

Do you want a Head Start in life? Do you want to know things that can make your life happier, easier, and more fulfilling? Or do you know someone in or out of school who you want to get the most out of their life?

201 Things You Need To Know About Life sets out easy to read information that can help the reader to:

- do more
- see more
- love more
- experience more, and
- get more of what they want in their life.

This book is for anyone who doesn't want to end up: not doing much in life, with no job or in a minimum wage job, married to someone they would rather not be with, or miserable that they didn't know things they should have known earlier in life that could have helped them to live life the way they truly want to live it.

Ever wonder if *you might be a Dickhead*? Maybe you aren't really sure what makes someone a Dickhead. Or maybe you aren't a Dickhead but you know someone who is, someone who doesn't realize that they are in fact a Dickhead, and you want them to know that they are.

If so, this book is for you.

Are You A Dickhead? takes a humorous but also educational look at manners and lack of manners. It looks at things that people do and don't do in Public, when Getting Around, in Relationships, and in their Brain that make them Dickheads.

Are You A Dickhead? asks the reader 100 simple questions and provides the reader with 5 circle the letter style simple multiple choice answers. By answering the questions, the reader is able to generate a score that enables the reader to determine if they are or are not in fact a Dickhead. If they are, they can make needed changes so that they aren't. Doing so makes the world a better place for us all.

Do the people you think are *friends* do or fail to do things that you expect a friend to not do or to do? Does it seem like they have forgotten what it means to be a *friend*? Or could it be that they don't have a clue what it takes to be a friend?

Do some of your *friends* get irritated, even upset with you for things you do or don't do? Could it be that you have forgotten or don't really know what it means or takes to be a friend?

If so, this book is for them, and you.

What Friends SHOULD Do takes a fun but serious look at 100 things real friends do and don't do. It looks at things that make someone a real friend, things such as: accepting us for who we really are, and telling us if we have a booger hanging out of our nose – when we do. Being a real friend and having real friends makes our life happier and better. Spending our time with people who aren't a real friend is a waste of our time – time that we could have used with people who are.

www.ingramcontent.com/pod-product-compliance
Lightning Source LLC
Chambersburg PA
CBHW070601010526
44118CB00012B/1410